EDUCATION, PARTICIPATION, AND POWER: ESSAYS IN THEORY AND PRACTICE

ROBERT C. RIORDAN
Introduction   1

HERBERT GINTIS
Toward a Political Economy of Education:
A Radical Critique of Ivan Illich's *Deschooling Society*   7

DENIS GOULET
An Ethical Model for the Study of Values   35

CENTER FOR NEW SCHOOLS
Strengthening Alternative High Schools   58

FRANK ADAMS
Highlander Folk School: Getting Information,
Going Back and Teaching It   96

ARTHUR E. THOMAS
Community Power and Student Rights:
An Interview with Arthur E. Thomas   120

EDUCATION, PARTICIPATION, AND POWER:
ESSAYS IN THEORY AND PRACTICE

with an introduction by
ROBERT C. RIORDAN

Harvard Educational Review
Reprint Series No. 10

Copyright © 1976 by President and Fellows of Harvard College.
All rights reserved. No part of this publication may be reproduced or transmitted in any form or by any means, electronic or mechanical, including photocopy, recording, or any information storage and retrieval system, without permission in writing from the publisher.

Library of Congress Card Number 76-433. ISBN 0-916690-01-6.
Printed by Capital City Press, Montpelier, Vermont 05602. Cover design by Cynthia Brady.

Harvard Educational Review
Longfellow Hall, 13 Appian Way
Cambridge, Massachusetts 02138

Introduction

Fundamental to these essays is what Paulo Freire calls an "option for man"; that is, an orientation which insists upon the vocation of man to transform the world according to his own purposes. Such a stance necessarily implies a commitment to human liberation—to a distribution of power whereby men and women participate interdependently in determining the direction of their lives. In education, this commitment calls for teachers and students alike to become conscious agents in a dynamic, mutual process of action and reflection rather than be mere passive transmitters and recipients of pre-packaged "knowledge."

Indeed, these articles may be read as an elaboration of Freire's basic theme in the context of North America.[1] Here I refer not simply to a method of adult literacy education, but to a historical, philosophical commitment with far-reaching implications. These articles invite and challenge us to become involved in the search for an unalienated methodology of transformative action, unalienated both in its insistence on a dynamic relationship between theory and practice, and in its restoration of the language and instruments of power (literacy, law, research technology) to the people. This is not idle sloganeering, for the significance of these articles is that they represent lived experiences which demonstrate that men and women can choose a hopeful future.

Freire's "option for man" is necessarily an option for change, for it is in the nature of man to become aware, to envision alternatives, and to transcend present limits. Educational structures and practices which promote this creative process are humanizing; those which inhibit it are dehumanizing. To choose the former requires a recognition that "there is no other road to humanization . . . but authen-

---

[1] In the case of Goulet and Thomas, there is a direct and explicit connection. With Gintis, Adams, and the Center for New Schools, it is implicit. All of these pieces appeared in the *Harvard Educational Review* within eighteen months after co-publication of Paulo Freire's monograph, *Cultural Action for Freedom* (1970) by the *Harvard Educational Review* and the Center for the Study of Development and Social Change.

tic transformation of the dehumanizing structure."[2] But how does change in educational settings relate to change in the larger society? What is the appropriate theoretical basis for a liberating education?

It is over this question of theory that Herbert Gintis confronts Ivan Illich's notion of "deschooling." Gintis argues that the proper context for projects in social transformation is within existing institutions. He also argues that the theoretical focus of such projects should be the social relations of production rather than patterns of consumption, since the former are the primary source of alienation in technologically advanced societies. In this view, work is not a mere occupation, but a vocation, through which men and women establish their relation to the world. Accordingly, the task in education is to develop a social structure wherein "individuals . . . exercise direct control over technology in structuring their various social environments, thereby developing and coming to understand their needs through their exercise of power."

Such a project is possible because, although the social relations of education mirror those of the larger society and vice versa, neither determine the other. Therefore it is feasible for men and women to orient themselves to a new vision even within the predominant social and economic reality. What is required is that parents, teachers, and students share a commitment to radically altered social relations which can only emerge through a continuing process of collective action and reflection. In other words, education must be both dialogical and dialectical, for the very task of defining a new model of social relations requires new and evolving modes of participation and interaction.

It is difficult, however, to abandon tradition, rules and regulations, and hierarchical social structure for uncertain momentary choices based on still-emerging values. Therein lies the enormous and complex responsibility of the educator who chooses humanization, for that choice requires continual reevaluation, clarification, and reaffirmation. This task is the subject of the remaining authors in this volume—Denis Goulet in a proposed research model, and the Center for New Schools, Frank Adams, and Arthur Thomas in reports on projects in institutional transformation.

Denis Goulet's context is the modern crisis in values as it confronts traditional societies undergoing rapid technological and social change. Since this is a crisis which continues to afflict the more developed nations, his research model is relevant to them as well.

[2] Paulo Freire, *Cultural Action for Freedom*, 1970.

Introduction
ROBERT C. RIORDAN

In Goulet's view, the study of values is properly a joint venture based on reciprocity between researchers and subjects, with outcomes accessible and useful to the subjects themselves. This view is at odds with conventional practices in social science research. Typically, it is social scientists and engineers alone who pose the questions, interpret the responses, and propose programs. Their training and expertise insulate them from their subjects, on whose lives their decisions may exert a large and unanswerable influence. For the subjects, this *vulnerability* is an experience and an expectation, generated in and by the social structure of domination. If the choice is for reciprocity, for mutual empowerment rather than control of one by the other, then researchers can authenticate that choice only by making themselves vulnerable to their subjects in turn. The validity of the research enterprise thus depends not only on the usual academic criteria, but also on the active collaboration and affirmation of knowing subjects.

Similar premises emerge from and are applied to a particular setting in the article from the Center for New Schools. "Strenthening Alternative Schools" offers a detailed and comprehensive analysis of the problems that confront persons who attempt to bring about fundamental change within a public school system. By no means are these problems solely attributable to characteristics of the system per se. Even more critical are the problems which arise within the alternative setting: conflicting priorities, ambivalence about leadership and group discipline, and the participants' prior internalization of conventional institutional values. Yet it is precisely these issues and influences which educators have a special responsibility to address.

This is the correct basis of the Center's critique of the faith in "organic development" which prevails in many alternative schools: not that an organic perspective is destructive in itself, but that educators may use it to avoid—or hide—uncomfortable choices.[3] The same criticism can be applied to a strictly mechanistic view. Although many students at Metro High School were reluctant to participate in governance mechanisms, it does not necessarily follow that they did not want to participate in critical decisions. Students may simply have perceived those mechanisms as inadequate to advance their interests. If a group of students organize themselves to protest a decision, make demands, or initiate a project, then power has been redistributed, even though the mechanisms may have failed. A broader view would recognize that potential exists for a process of conflict, negotiation, and

---

[3] Faith in "organic development" refers to the uncritical assumption that new and desirable patterns of thought and behavior will evolve naturally once traditional institutional constraints are removed.

resolution apart from governance structures, or at least that students' responses to critical issues may be more important than their responses to mechanisms.

As the Center demonstrates in its later general analysis, it is both possible and necessary to make explicit the relationship between specific issues and basic group commitments. Behind the mechanisms, and behind what happens organically, lies a prior, yet problematic, choice. Analysis of structures, events, and situations should proceed from and return to that choice. A commitment to empowerment, for example, demands that issues and mechanisms not be separated; it asks not only "what forms of student participation most closely model the distribution and exercise of power in the ideal society?" but also "what are the crucial decisions here that affect students' lives?" And from there, "what next step will take us closest to the concrete realization of dynamic, democratic social relations in this setting?" Research may illuminate such issues, but it cannot determine their resolution. That is, research cannot remove the educators' and students' collective burden of choice, which increases rather than decreases as one moves away from conventional practices.

The Center for New Schools forcefully articulates the need for alternative schools to clarify goals and priorities and develop positive alternative practices. Certainly its analysis of student involvement at Metro is cast in an affirmative framework. Yet in this instance, the focus on student response to mechanisms leads to a negation, i.e., to the explanation of a "failure." Such an analysis, although instructive, is incomplete. We also need to understand those more successful moments, rare or isolated as they may seem, when vision and reality merge—such as the moments when Metro's all-school meeting did work. What were the issues, what happened, what was present then that was not at other times? What is lost in the assertion that "the all-school meeting failed"?[4]

We need to appreciate the value of "sufficient moments,"—of real events or situations in the life of a setting which are sufficient (1) to illustrate the affirmative resolution of a critical issue, and (2) to sustain the belief which underlies the effort to transform dehumanizing structures. These are moments when the potential for transformation is revealed and realized and when we are reminded, despite our setbacks, that modest projects motivated by genuine commitment may indeed promote change in contiguous structures and in the larger society. What can we under-

---

[4] I would stress that this is a specific, not a general, criticism. The Center for New Schools has taken major strides in the development and dissemination of successful practices, affirmative research techniques, and useful technical assistance strategies.

Introduction
ROBERT C. RIORDAN

stand of these moments of clarity when principles and practice illuminate each other?

Frank Adams and Arthur Thomas describe such moments at the Highlander Folk School and the Center for the Study of Student Citizenship, Rights, and Responsibilities. At Highlander, Miles Horton not only models what Goulet would call reciprocity and vulnerability, but also recognizes the need to withhold his "expertise" at a critical moment so that control over that moment may be vested in the workers. At the Dayton Center, a parent ombudsman discovers and uses an Ohio statute on school expulsions. These moments bear witness to what is possible when persons are encouraged to participate in transformative action.

Indeed, what is distinctive about Art Thomas's richly anecdotal interview is its quality of witness. Thomas projects a hopeful vision because he has experienced such moments—when things which were dreamed, happen. In this way "sufficient moments" have an instrumental value: as part of the folklore of a setting, they confirm a positive, optimistic-though-critical vision, which in turn increases the potential for transformation. Thomas's choice is to affirm that such moments can happen consistently, and to work to that end.

Thomas' work is close to Paulo Freire's in both aim and method. In each case, the subject matter (law or literacy) is proposed as a liberating technology. The basic issue is control over one's own destiny, and the approach is through demystification, action, and reflection. Through discussion of real and prototypical events and situations in their own lives, participants are encouraged not only to develop skills, but also to discover and confront the sources of their alienation. Students at the Dayton Center experience the control and dignity that can come from knowledge of how to use the law in the way that Freire's students experience the same from learning to "make words speak."

Indeed, Thomas's mode is plain speaking: "It's a matter of loving, trusting, and respecting the people and it's a matter of doing *with* rather than *for* the people." His experience, accessible to us through the moments he describes, gives substance to those words. An analysis which ignores such language and moments misses the essence of humanizing projects. It is not enough to dismiss the successes of the Dayton Center or the Highlander Folk School as reflecting the idiosyncracies of a single charismatic figure. Nor is it useful to attempt to devise the ultimate mechanism—the teacher-proof curriculum, the conflict-free setting—which would work its effect independent of human responsibility and choice. In such mechanistic projects, which are in effect no more than dehumanizing schemes, we hide our prior choices and disown the fundamental responsibility of both teacher and learner.

There is no escaping that responsibility in a project which opts for man. There is no other way out of dehumanizing structures than to model new patterns of behavior in their midst.

It is not surprising that the Center for New Schools, Frank Adams, and Art Thomas report formidable psychological, social, and political barriers to institutional transformation. Nor is it surprising that these barriers develop at the heart of such projects. For the conflicts are inevitable: ideals versus necessity, individual versus collective action, new aims versus prior socialization. That is why the central problem in such settings is to generate a shared set of principles and a shared theory which goes beyond the unidimensional, materialistic conception of man and social relations that pervades modern institutional life. Again, the crux is commitment, not to a predetermined technique, strategy, or ideology, but to existential choices, reaffirmed in day-to-day practice, and to a methodology which is at once scientific and philosophical, pragmatic and utopian, rational and spiritual.

The theory and practice described in this volume form part of a conscious effort to forge such a methodology—concretely situated, dialogical, dialectical, and committed to awareness and action—which proposes human liberation in direct opposition to dehumanizing structures. The shape of that methodology is discernible not only in theoretical reflections, but also in portraits of concrete moments—in the structure of those moments and the commitment which activates them. There are enough models and moments to sustain us. Above all, however, there is the necessity to choose. Thomas says, "the children, if we allow them, will lead the way." Allowing them means struggling to transform dehumanizing institutional structures. For if we share a commitment to an alternative vision, then we also share the long, arduous task of making it so.

ROBERT C. RIORDAN

Toward a Political Economy of Education: A Radical Critique of *Ivan Illich's* Deschooling Society

HERBERT GINTIS

Harvard University

The author critiques Ivan Illich's Deschooling Society, *arguing that, despite his forthright vision of the liberating potential of educational technology, Illich fails to understand fully how the existing educational system serves the capitalist economy. Gintis evaluates and rejects the book's major thesis that the present character of schooling stems from the economy's need to shape consumer demands and expectations. Instead, he offers a production orientation which maintains that the repressive and unequal aspects of schooling derive from the need to supply a labor force compatible with the social relations of capitalist production. Gintis concludes that meaningful strategies for educational change must explicitly embrace a concomitant transformation of the mechanisms of power and privilege in the economic sphere.*

Ivan Illich's *Deschooling Society*, despite its bare 115 pages, embraces the world. Its ostensible focus on education moves him inexorably and logically through the panoply of human concerns in advanced industrial society—a society plainly in

---

* Ivan Illich, *Deschooling Society* (New York: Harper & Row, 1971). The ideas in this paper were developed in cooperation with Samuel Bowles, whose help in preparing this manuscript was integral. For a more detailed discussion of the theoretical and historical issues raised in this paper see Samuel Bowles and Herbert Gintis, *Schooling in Capitalist America: Educational Reform and the Contradictions of Economic Life* (New York: Basic Books, 1975).

progressive disintegration and decay. With Yeats we may feel that "things fall apart/ The center cannot hold," but Illich's task is no less than to discover and analyze that "center." His endeavor affords the social scientist the unique and rare privilege to put in order the historical movements which characterize our age and define the prospects for a revolutionary future. Such is the subject of this essay.

This little book would have been unthinkable ten years ago. In it, Ivan Illich confronts the full spectrum of the modern crisis in values by rejecting the basic tenets of progressive liberalism. He dismisses what he calls the Myth of Consumption as a cruel and illusory ideology foisted upon the populace by a manipulative bureaucratic system. He treats welfare and service institutions as part of the problem, not as part of the solution. He rejects the belief that education constitutes the "great equalizer" and the path to personal liberation. Schools, say Illich, simply must be eliminated.

Illich does more than merely criticize; he conceptualizes constructive technological alternatives to repressive education. Moreover, he sees the present age as "revolutionary" because the existing social relations of economic and political life, including the dominant institutional structure of schooling, have become impediments to the development of liberating, socially productive technologies. Here Illich is relevant indeed, for the tension between technological possibility and social reality pervades all advanced industrial societies today. Despite our technological power, communities and environment continue to deteriorate, poverty and inequality persist, work remains alienating, and men and women are not liberated for self-fulfilling activity.

Illich's response is a forthright vision of participatory, decentralized, and liberating learning technologies, and a radically altered vision of social relations in education.

Yet, while his *description* of modern society is sufficiently critical, his *analysis* is simplistic and his program, consequently, is a diversion from the immensely complex and demanding political, organizational, intellectual, and personal demands of revolutionary reconstruction in the coming decades. It is crucial that educators and students who have been attracted to him—for his message does correspond to their personal frustration and disillusionment—move beyond him.

The first part of this essay presents Illich's analysis of the economically advanced society—the basis for his analysis of schools. Whereas Illich locates the source of the social problems and value crises of modern societies in their need to reproduce alienated patterns of *consumption,* I argue that these patterns are merely manifestations of the deeper workings of the economic system. The second part of the

A Radical Critique of Ivan Illich
HERBERT GINTIS

essay attempts to show that Illich's over-emphasis on consumption leads him to a very partial understanding of the functions of the educational system and the contradictions presently besetting it, and hence to ineffective educational alternatives and untenable political strategies for the implementation of desirable educational technologies.

Finally, I argue that a radical theory of educational reform becomes viable only by envisioning liberating and equal education as serving and being served by a radically altered nexus of social relations in *production*. Schools may lead or lag in this process of social transformation, but structural changes in the educational process can be socially relevant only when they speak to potentials for liberation and equality in our day-to-day labors. In the final analysis "de-schooling" is irrelevant because we cannot "de-factory," "de-office," or "de-family," save perhaps at the still unenvisioned end of a long process of social reconstruction.

The Social Context of Modern Schooling: Institutionalized Values and Commodity Fetishism

Educational reformers commonly err by treating the system of schools as if it existed in a social vacuum. Illich does not make this mistake. Rather, he views the internal irrationalities of modern education as reflections of the larger society. The key to understanding the problems of advanced industrial economies, he argues, lies in the character of its consumption activities and the ideology which supports them. The schools in turn are exemplary models of bureaucracies geared toward the indoctrination of docile and manipulable consumers.

Guiding modern social life and interpersonal behavior, says Illich, is a destructive system of "institutionalized values" which determine how one perceives one's needs and defines instruments for their satisfaction. The process which creates institutional values insures that all individual needs—physical, psychological, social, intellectual, emotional, and spiritual—are transformed into demands for goods and services. In contrast to the "psychological impotence" which results from institutionalized values, Illich envisages the "psychic health" which emerges from self-realization—both personal and social. Guided by institutionalized values, one's well-being lies not in what one *does* but in what one *has*—the status of one's job and the level of material consumption. For the active person, goods are merely means to or instruments in the performance of activities; for the passive consumer, however, goods are ends in themselves, and activity is merely the means toward sustaining or displaying a desired level of consumption. Thus institutionalized values manifest themselves psychologically in a rigorous fetishism—in this case, of commodities and public services. Illich's vision rests in the negation of commodity fetishism[1]:

> I believe that a desirable future depends on our deliberately . . . engendering a life style which will enable us to be spontaneous, independent, yet related to each other, rather than maintaining a life style which only allows us to make and unmake, produce and consume. (*Deschooling Society*, hereafter *DS*, p. 52)

Commodity fetishism is institutionalized in two senses. First, the "delivery systems" in modern industrial economies (i.e., the suppliers of goods and services) are huge, bureaucratic institutions which treat individuals as mere receptors for their products. Goods are supplied by hierarchical and impersonal corporate enterprises, while services are provided by welfare bureaucracies which enjoy ". . . a professional, political and financial monopoly over the social imagination, setting standards of what is valuable and what is feasible. . . . A whole society is initiated into the Myth of Unending Consumption of services" (*DS*, p. 44).

Second, commodity fetishism is institutionalized in the sense that the values of passive consumerism are induced and reinforced by the same "delivery systems" whose ministrations are substitutes for self-initiated activities.

> . . . manipulative institutions . . . are either socially or psychologically 'addictive.' Social addiction . . . consists in the tendency to prescribe increased treatment if smaller quantities have not yielded the desired results. Psychological addiction . . . results when consumers become hooked on the need for more and more of the process or product. (*DS*, p. 55)

These delivery systems moreover "both invite compulsively repetitive use and frustrate alternative ways of achieving similar results." For example, General Motors and Ford

> . . . produce means of transportation, but they also, and more importantly, manipulate public taste in such a way that the need for transportation is expressed as a demand for private cars rather than public buses. They sell the desire to control a machine, to race at high speeds in luxurious comfort, while also offering the fantasy at the end of the road. (*DS*, p. 57)

---

[1] Illich himself does not use the term "commodity fetishism." I shall do so, however, as it is more felicitous than "institutionalized values" in many contexts.

A Radical Critique of Ivan Illich
HERBERT GINTIS

This analysis of addictive manipulation in private production is, of course, well-developed in the literature.[2] Illich's contribution is to extend it to the sphere of service and welfare bureaucracies:

> Finally, teachers, doctors, and social workers realize that their distinct professional ministrations have one aspect—at least—in common. They create further demands for the institutional treatments they provide, faster than they can provide service institutions. (*DS*, p. 112)

The well-socialized naturally react to these failures simply by increasing the power and jurisdiction of welfare institutions. Illich's reaction, of course, is precisely the contrary.

The Political Response to Institutionalized Values

As the basis for his educational proposals, Illich's overall framework bears close attention. Since commodity fetishism is basically a psychological stance, it must first be attacked on an individual rather than political level. For Illich, each individual is responsible for his/her own demystification. The institutionalization of values occurs not through external coercion, but through psychic manipulation, so its rejection is an apolitical act of individual will. The movement for social change thus becomes a cultural one of raising consciousness.

But even on this level, political action in the form of *negating* psychic manipulation is crucial. Goods and services as well as welfare bureaucracies must be *prohibited* from disseminating fetishistic values. Indeed, this is the basis for a political program of de-schooling. The educational system, as a coercive source of institutionalized values, must be denied its preferred status. Presumably, this "politics of negation" would extend to advertising and all other types of psychic manipulation.

Since the concrete social manifestation of commodity fetishism is a grossly inflated level of production and consumption, the second step in Illich's political program is the substitution of leisure for work. Work is evil for Illich—unrewarding by its very nature—and not to be granted the status of "activity":

> ... 'making and acting' are different, so different, in fact, that one never includes the

---

[2] See, for instance, Herbert Gintis, "Consumer Behavior and the Concept of Sovereignty: Explanation of Social Decay," *American Economic Review*, 62 (May 1972), 267-278; Gintis, "Welfare Economics and Individual Development," *Quarterly Journal of Economics* 86 (November 1972), 572-599; John K. Galbraith, *The New Industrial State* (Boston: Houghton Mifflin, 1963); Herbert Marcuse, *One Dimensional Man* (Boston: Beacon Press, 1964).

other. . . . Modern technology has increased the ability of man to relinquish the 'making' of things to machines, and his potential time for 'acting' has increased. . . . Unemployment is the sad idleness of a man who, contrary to Aristotle, believes that making things, or working, is virtuous and that idleness is bad. (*DS*, p. 62)

Again, Illich's shift in the work-leisure choice is basically apolitical and will follow naturally from the abolition of value indoctrination. People work so hard and long because they are taught to believe the fruits of their activities—consumption—are intrinsically worthy. Elimination of the "hard-sell pitch" of bureaucratic institutions will allow individuals to discover *within themselves* the falsity of the doctrine.

The third stage in Illich's political program envisages the necessity of concrete change in social "delivery systems." Manipulative institutions must be *dismantled*, to be replaced by organizational forms which allow for the free development of individuals. Illich calls such institutions "convivial," and associates them with leftist political orientation.

The regulation of convivial institutions sets limits to their use; as one moves from the convivial to the manipulative end of the spectrum, the rules progressively call for unwilling consumption or participation. . . . Toward, but not at, the left on the institutional spectrum, we can locate enterprises which compete with others in their own field, but have not begun notably to engage in advertising. Here we find hand laundries, small bakeries, hairdressers, and—to speak of professionals—some lawyers and music teachers. . . . They acquire clients through their personal touch and the comparative quality of their services. (*DS*, p. 55-6)

In short, Illich's Good Society is based on small scale entrepreneurial (as opposed to corporate) capitalism, with perfectly competitive markets in goods and services. The role of the state in this society is the prevention of manipulative advertising, the development of left-convivial technologies compatible with self-initiating small-group welfare institutions (education, health and medical services, crime prevention and rehabilitation, community development, etc.) and the provisioning of the social infrastructure (e.g., public transportation). Illich's proposal for "learning webs" in education is only a particular application of this vision of left-convivial technologies.

Assessing Illich's Politics: An Overview

Illich's model of consumption-manipulation is crucial at every stage of his political argument. But it is substantially incorrect. In the following three sections I shall criticize three basic thrusts of his analysis.

A Radical Critique of Ivan Illich
HERBERT GINTIS

First, Illich locates the source of social decay in the autonomous, manipulative behavior of corporate bureaucracies. I shall argue, in contrast, that the source must be sought in the normal operation of the basic *economic* institutions of capitalism (markets in factors of production, private control of resources and technology, etc.),[3] which consistently sacrifice the healthy development of community, work, environment, education, and social equality to the accumulation of capital and the growth of marketable goods and services. Moreover, given that individuals must participate in economic activity, these social outcomes are quite insensitive to the preferences or values of individuals, and are certainly in no sense a reflection of the autonomous wills of manipulating bureaucrats or gullible consumers. Hence merely ending "manipulation" while maintaining basic economic institutions will affect the rate of social decay only minimally.

Second, Illich locates the *source* of consumer consciousness in the manipulative socialization of individuals by agencies controlled by corporate and welfare bureaucracies. This "institutionalized consciousness" induces indivduals to choose outcomes not in conformity with their "real" needs. I shall argue, in contrast, that a causal analysis can *never* take socialization agencies as basic explanatory variables in assessing the overall behavior of the social system.[4] In particular, consumer consciousness is generated through *the day-to-day activities and observations* of individuals in capitalist society. The sales pitches of manipulative institutions, rather than *generating* the values of commodity fetishism, merely *capitalize* upon and *reinforce* a set of values derived from and reconfirmed by daily personal experience in the social system. In fact, while consumer behavior may seem irrational and fetishistic, it is a reasonable accommodation to the options for meaningful social outlets *in the context* of capitalist institutions. Hence the abolition of addictive propaganda cannot "liberate" the individual to "free choice" of personal goals. Such choice is still conditioned by the pattern of social processes which have historically rendered him or her amenable to "institutionalized values." In fact, the likely outcome of de-manipulation of values would be no significant alteration of values at all.

[3] Throughout this paper, I restrict my analysis to *capitalist* as opposed to other economic systems of advanced industrial societies (e.g., state-socialism of the Soviet Union type). As Illich suggests, the *outcomes* are much the same, but the *mechanisms* are in fact quite different. The private-administrative economic power of a capitalist elite is mirrored by the public-administrative political power of a bureaucratic elite in state-socialist countries, and both are used to reproduce a similar complex of social relations of production and a structurally equivalent system of class relations. The capitalist variety is emphasized here because of its special relevance in the American context.

[4] Gintis, "Consumer Behavior and the Concept of Sovereignty."

Moreover, the ideology of commodity fetishism not only *reflects* the day-to-day operations of the economic system, it is also *functionally necessary* to motivate men/women to accept and participate in the system of alienated production, to peddle their (potentially) creative activities to the highest bidder through the market in labor, to accept the destruction of their communities, and to bear allegiance to an economic system whose market institutions and patterns of control of work and community systematically subordinate all social goals to the criteria of profit and marketable product. Thus the weakening of institutionalized values would in itself lead logically either to unproductive and undirected social chaos (witness the present state of counter-culture movements in the United States) or to a rejection of the social relations of capitalist production along with commodity fetishism.

Third, Illich argues that the goal of social change is to transform institutions according to the criterion of "non-addictiveness," or "left-conviviality." However, since manipulation and addictiveness are not the sources of social decay, their elimination offers no cure. Certainly the implementation of left-convivial forms in welfare and service agencies—however desirable in itself—will not counter the effects of capitalist development on social life. More important, Illich's criterion explicitly accepts those basic economic institutions which structure decision-making power, lead to the growth of corporate and welfare bureaucracies, and lie at the root of social decay. Thus Illich's criterion must be replaced by one of democratic, participatory, and rationally decentralized control over social outcomes in factory, office, community, schools, and media. The remainder of this essay will elucidate the alternative analysis and political strategy as focused on the particular case of the educational system.

Economic Institutions and Social Development

In line with Illich's suggestion, we may equate individual welfare with the pattern of day-to-day *activities* the individual enters into, together with the personal *capacities*—physical, cognitive, affective, spiritual, and aesthetic—he or she has developed toward their execution and appreciation. Most individual activity is not purely personal, but is based on social interaction and requires a social setting conducive to developing the relevant capacities for performance. That is, activities take place within socially structured domains, characterized by legitimate and socially acceptable roles available to the individual in social relations. The most

A Radical Critique of Ivan Illich
HERBERT GINTIS

important of these activity contexts are work, community, and natural environment. The character of individual participation in these contexts—the defining roles one accepts as worker and community member and the way one relates to one's environment—is a basic determinant of well-being and individual development.

These activity contexts, as I shall show, are structured in turn by the way people structure their *productive relations*. The study of activity contexts in capitalist society must begin with an understanding of the basic economic institutions which regulate their historical development.

The most important of these institutions are: 1) *private ownership* of factors of production (land, labor, and capital), according to which the owner has full control over their disposition and development; 2) *a market in labor*, according to which a) the worker is divorced, by and large, from ownership of non-human factors of production (land and capital), b) the worker relinquishes control over the disposition of his labor during the stipulated workday by exchanging it for money, and c) the price of a particular type of labor (skilled or unskilled, white-collar or blue-collar, physical, mental, managerial, or technical) is determined essentially by supply and demand; 3) a *market in land*, according to which the price of each parcel of land is determined by supply and demand, and the use of such parcels is individually determined by the highest bidder; 4) income determination on the basis of the *market-dictated returns to owned factors* of production; 5) *markets in essential commodities*—food, shelter, social insurance, medical care; and 6) *control of the productive process by owners of capital* or their managerial representatives.[5]

Because essential goods, services, and activity contexts are marketed, income is a prerequisite to social existence. Because factors of production are privately owned and market-determined factor returns are the legitimate source of income, and because most workers possess little more than their own labor services, they are required to provide these services to the economic system. Thus control over the developing of work roles and of the social technology of production passes into the hands of the representatives of capital.

Thus the activity context of work becomes alienated in the sense that its structure and historical development do not conform to the needs of the individuals it affects.[6] Bosses determine the technologies and social relations of production within

---

[5] The arguments in this section are presented at greater length in Gintis, "Power and Alienation," in *Modern Political Economy*, ed. James Weaver (Rockleigh, N. J.: Allyn and Bacon, 1972) and Gintis, "Consumer Behavior and the Concept of Sovereignty."

[6] This definition conforms to Marxist usage in that "alienation" refers to *social processes*, not psychological states. For some discussion of this term in Marxist literature, see Gintis, "Power and Alienation," and Gintis, "Consumer Behavior and the Concept of Sovereignty."

the enterprise on the basis of three criteria. First, production must be flexibly organized for decision-making and secure managerial control from the highest levels downward. This means generally that technologies employed must be compatible with hierarchical authority and a fragmented, task-specific division of labor.[7] The need to maintain effective administrative power leads to bureaucratic order in production, the hallmark of modern corporate organization. Second, among all technologies and work roles compatible with secure and flexible control from the top, bosses choose those which minimize costs and maximize profits. Finally, bosses determine product attributes—and hence the "craft rationality" of production—according to their contribution to gross sales and growth of the enterprise. Hence the decline in pride of workmanship and quality of production associated with the Industrial Revolution.

There is no reason to believe that a great deal of desirable work is not possible. On the contrary, evidence indicates that decentralization, worker control, the reintroduction of craft in production, job rotation, and the elimination of the most constraining aspects of hierarchy are both feasible and potentially efficient. But such work roles develop in an institutional context wherein control, profit, and growth regulate the development of the social relations of production. Unalienated production must be the result of the revolutionary transformation of the basic institutions which Illich implicitly accepts.

The development of communities as activity contexts also must be seen in terms of basic economic institutions. The market in land, by controlling the organic development of communities, not only produces the social, environmental, and aesthetic monstrosities we call "metropolitan areas," but removes from the community the creative, synthesizing power that lies at the base of true solidarity. Thus communities become agglomerates of isolated individuals with few common activities and impersonal and apathetic interpersonal relations.

A community cannot thrive when it holds no effective power over the autonomous activities of profit-maximizing capitalists. Rather, a true community is *itself* a creative, initiating, and synthesizing agent, with the power to determine the architectural unity of its living and working spaces and their coordination, the power to allocate community property to social uses such as participatory child-care and community recreation centers, and the power to insure the preservation and development of its natural ecological environment. This is not an idle utopian dream. Many living-working communities do exhibit architectural, aesthetic, social, and

[7] See the essay by Stephen Marglin, "What Do Bosses Do?" *Review of Radical Political Economics,* 6 (Summer 1974), 60-112.

A Radical Critique of Ivan Illich
HERBERT GINTIS

ecological integrity: the New England town, the Dutch village, the moderate-sized cities of Mali in sub-Saharan Africa, and the desert communities of Djerba in Tunisia. True, these communities are fairly static and untouched by modern technology; but even in a technologically advanced country the potential for decent community is great, given the proper pattern of community decision mechanisms.

The normal operation of the basic economic institutions of capitalism thus render major activity contexts inhospitable to human beings. Our analysis of work and community could easily be extended to include ecological environment and economic equality with similar conclusions.[8]

This analysis undermines Illich's treatment of public service bureaucracies. Illich holds that service agencies (including schools) fail because they are manipulative, and expand because they are psychologically addictive. In fact, they do not fail at all. And they expand because they exist as integral links in the larger institutional allocation of unequal power and income. Illich's simplistic treatment of this area is illustrated in his explanation for the expansion of military operations:

> The boomerang effect in war is becoming more obvious: the higher the body count of dead Vietnamese, the more enemies the United States acquires around the world; likewise, the more the United States must spend to create another manipulative institution—cynically dubbed 'pacification'—in a futile effort to absorb the side effects of war. (*DS,* p. 54)

Illich's theory of addiction as motivation proposes that, once begun, one thing naturally leads to another. Actually, however, the purpose of the military is the maintenance of aggregate demand and high levels of employment, as well as aiding the expansion of international sources of resource supply and capital investment. Expansion is not the result of addiction but a primary characteristic of the entire system.[9]

Likewise from a systematic point of view, penal, mental illness, and poverty agencies are meant to contain the dislocations arising from the fragmentation of work and community and the institutionally determined inequality in income and power. Yet Illich argues only:

> ... jail increases both the quality and the quantity of criminals, that, in fact, it often creates them out of mere nonconformists ... mental hospitals, nursing homes, and orphan asylums do much the same thing. These institutions provide their clients with the destructive self-

---

[8] See Michael Reich and David Finkelhor, "The Military-Industrial Complex," in *The Capitalist System,* ed. Richard C. Edwards, Michael Reich, and Thomas Weisskopf (New York: Prentice-Hall, 1972).

[9] See Gintis, "Power and Alienation," for a concise summary.

image of the psychotic, the overaged, or the waif, and provide a rationale for the existence of entire professions, just as jails produce income for wardens. (*DS*, p. 54)

Further, the cause of expansion of service agencies lies *not* in their addictive nature, but in their failure even to attempt to deal with the institutional sources of social problems. The normal operation of basic economic institutions progressively aggravates these problems, hence requiring increased response on the part of welfare agencies.

The Roots of Consumer Behavior

To understand consumption in capitalist society requires a *production* orientation, in contrast to Illich's emphasis on "institutionalized values" as basic explanatory variables. Individuals consume as they do—and hence acquire values and beliefs concerning consumption—because of the place consumption activity holds among the constellation of available alternatives for social expression. These alternatives directly involve the quality of basic activity contexts surrounding social life—contexts which, as I have argued, develop according to the criteria of capital accumulation through the normal operation of economic institutions.

What at first glance seems to be an irrational preoccupation with income and consumption in capitalist society, is seen within an activity context paradigm to be a logical response on the part of the individual to what Marx isolated as the central tendency of capitalist society: the transformation of all complex social relations into impersonal *quid-pro-quo* relations. One implication of this transformation is the progressive decay of social activity contexts described in the previous section, a process which reduces their overall contribution to individual welfare. Work, community, and environment become sources of pain and displeasure rather than inviting contexts for social relations. The reasonable individual response, then, is a) to disregard the development of personal capacities which would be humanly satisfying in activity contexts which are not available and, hence, to fail to demand changed activity contexts and b) to emphasize consumption and to develop those capacities which are most relevant to consumption *per se*.

Second, the transformation of complex social relations to exchange relations implies that the dwindling stock of healthy activity contexts is parceled out among individuals almost strictly according to income. High-paying jobs are by and large the least alienating; the poor live in the most fragmented communities and are subjected to the most inhuman environments; contact with natural environment

A Radical Critique of Ivan Illich
HERBERT GINTIS

is limited to periods of *vacation*, and the length and desirability of this contact is based on the means to pay.

Thus commodity fetishism becomes a *substitute* for meaningful activity contexts, and a *means of access* to those that exist. The "sales pitch" of Madison Avenue is accepted because, in the given context, it is true. It may not be much, but it's all we've got. The indefensibility of its more extreme forms (e.g., susceptibility to deodorant and luxury automobile advertising) should not divert us from comprehending this essential rationality.

In conclusion, it is clear that the motivational basis of consumer behavior derives from the everyday observation and experience of individuals, and consumer values are not "aberrations" induced by manipulative socialization. Certainly there is no reason to believe that individuals would consume or work much less were manipulative socialization removed. Insofar as such socialization is required to *stabilize* commodity fetishist values, its elimination might lead to the overthrow of capitalist *institutions*—but that of course is quite outside Illich's scheme.

The Limitations of Left-Convivial Technologies

Since Illich views the "psychological impotence" of the individual in his/her "addictedness" to the ministrations of corporate and state bureaucracies as the basic problem of contemporary society, he defines the desirable "left-convivial" institutions by the criterion of "non-addictiveness."

Applied to commodities or welfare services, this criterion is perhaps sufficient. But applied to major contexts of social activities, it is inappropriate. It is not possible for individuals to treat their work, their communities, and their environment in a simply instrumental manner. For better or worse, these social spheres, by regulating the individual's social activity, became a major determinant of his/her psychic development, and in an important sense define *who* he/she is. Indeed, the solution to the classical "problem of order" in society[10] is solved only by the individual's becoming "addicted" to his/her social forms by *participating through them*.[11] In remaking society, individuals do more than expand their freedom of choice—they change *who they are*, their self-definition, in the process. The criticism of alienated social spheres is not simply that they deprive individuals of necessary

---

[10] Talcott Parsons, *The Structure of Social Action* (New York: Free Press, 1939).
[11] Karl Marx, *The Economic and Philosophical Manuscripts of 1844* (Moscow: Foreign Language Publishing House, 1959) and Karl Marx and Friedrich Engels, *The Germany Ideology* (New York: International Publishers, 1947).

instruments of activity, but that in so doing they tend to produce in all of us something less than *we intend to be*.

The irony of Illich's analysis is that by erecting "addictiveness vs. instrumentality" as the central welfare criterion, he himself assumes a commodity fetishist mentality. In essence, he posits the individual *outside* of society and using social forms as instruments in his/her preexisting ends. For instance, Illich does not speak of work as "addictive," because in fact individuals treat work first as a "disutility" and second as an instrument toward other ends (consumption). The alienation of work poses no threat to the "sovereignty" of the worker because he is not addicted to it. By definition, then, capitalist work, communities, and environments are "nonaddictive" and left-convivial. Illich's consideration of the capitalist enterprise as "right-manipulative" only with respect to the consumer is a perfect example of this "reification" of the social world. In contrast, I would argue that work is *necessarily addictive* in the larger sense of determining who a man/woman is as a human being.

The addictive vs. instrumental (or, equivalently, manipulative vs. convivial) criterion is relevant only if we posit an essential "human nature" prior to social experience. Manipulation can then be seen as the perversion of the natural essence of the individual, and the de-institutionalization of values allows the individual to return to his/her essential self for direction. But the concept of the individual prior to society is nonsense. All individuals are concrete persons, uniquely developed through their particular articulation with social life.

The poverty of Illich's "addictiveness" criterion is dramatized in his treatment of technology. While he correctly recognizes that technology can be developed for purposes of either repression or liberation, his conception requires that the correct unalienated development of technological and institutional forms will follow from a simple aggregation of individual preferences over "left-convivial" alternatives.

The same analysis which I applied to the atomistic aggregation of preferences in the determination of activity contexts applies here as well: there is no reason to believe that ceding control of technological innovation and diffusion to a few, while rendering them subject to market criteria of success and failure, will produce desirable outcomes. Indeed this is *precisely* the mechanism operative in the private capitalist economy, with demonstrably adverse outcomes. According to the criterion of left-conviviality, the historical development of technology in *both* private and public spheres will conform to criteria of profitability and entrepreneurial control. Citizens are reduced to *passive consumers*, picking and choosing among the technological alternatives a technological elite presents to them.

A Radical Critique of Ivan Illich
HERBERT GINTIS

In contrast, it seems clear to me that individuals must exercise direct control over technology in structuring their various social environments, thereby developing and coming to understand their needs through their exercise of power. The control of technical and institutional forms must be vested directly in the group of individuals involved in a social activity, else the alienation of these individuals from one another becomes a *postulate* of the technical and institutional development of this social activity—be it in factory, office, school, or community.

In summary, the facile criterion of left-conviviality must be replaced by the less immediate—but correct—criterion of *unalienated social outcomes*: the institutionally mediated allocation of power must be so ordered that social outcomes conform to the wills and needs of participating individuals, and the quality of participation must be such as to promote the full development of individual capacities for self-understanding and social effectiveness.

Schooling: The Pre-Alienation of Docile Consumers

Everywhere the hidden curriculum of schooling initiates the citizen to the myth that bureaucracies guided by scientific knowledge are efficient and benevolent.... And everywhere it develops the habit of self-defeating consumption of services and alienating production, the tolerance for institutional dependence, and the recognition of institutional rankings. (*DS*, p. 74)

Illich sets his analysis of the educational system squarely on its strategic position in reproducing the economic relations of the larger society. While avoiding the inanity of reformers, who see "liberated education" as compatible with current capitalist political and economic institutions, he rejects the rigidity of old-style revolutionaries, who would see even more repressive (though different) education as a tool in forging "socialist consciousness" in the Workers' State.

What less perceptive educators have viewed as irrational, mean, and petty in modern schooling, Illich views as merely reflecting the operation of all manipulative institutions. In the first place, he argues, the educational system takes its place alongside other service bureaucracies, selling a manipulative, pre-packaged product, rendering their services addictive, and monopolizing all alternatives to self-initiated education on the part of individuals and small consenting groups.

Yet, argues Illich, schools cannot possibly achieve their goal of promoting learning. For as in every dimension of human experience, learning is the result of personal *activity*, not professional ministration:

Most learning is not the result of instruction. It is rather the result of unhampered participation in a meaningful setting. Most people learn best by being 'with it,' yet school makes them identify their personal, cognitive growth with elaborate planning and manipulation. (*DS,* p. 39)

Thus, as with all bureaucratic service institutions, schools fail by their very nature. And true to form, the more they fail, the more reliance is placed on them, and the more they expand:

Everywhere in the world school costs have risen faster than enrollments and faster than the GNP, everywhere expenditures on school fall even further behind the expectations of parents, teachers, and pupils.... School gives unlimited opportunity for legitimated waste, so long as its destructiveness goes unrecognized and the cost of palliatives goes up. (*DS,* p. 10)

From the fact that schools do not promote learning, however, Illich does not conclude that schools are simply irrational or discardable. Rather, he asserts their central role in creating docile and manipulable consumers for the larger society. For just as these men and women are defined by the quality of their *possessions* rather than of their *activities,* so they must learn to "transfer responsibility from self to institutions...."

Once a man or woman has accepted the need for school, he or she is easy prey for other institutions. Once young people have allowed their imaginations to be formed by curricular instruction, they are conditioned to institutional planning of every sort. 'Instruction' smothers the horizon of their imaginations. (*DS,* p. 39)

Equally they learn that anything worthwhile is standardized, certified, and can be purchased.

Even more lamentable, repressive schooling forces commodity fetishism on individuals by thwarting their development of personal capacities for autonomous and initiating social activity:

People who have been schooled down to size let unmeasured experience slip out of their hands.... They do not have to be robbed of their creativity. Under instruction, they have unlearned to 'do' their thing or 'be' themselves, and value only what has been made or could be made.... (*DS,* p. 40)

Recent research justifies Illich's emphasis on the "hidden curriculum" of schooling. Mass public education has not evolved into its present bureaucratic, hierarchical, and authoritarian form because of the organizational prerequisites of imparting cognitive skills. Such skills may in fact be more efficiently developed in demo-

A Radical Critique of Ivan Illich
HERBERT GINTIS

cratic, non-repressive atmospheres.[12] Rather, the social relations of education produce and reinforce those values, attitudes, and affective capacities which allow individuals to move smoothly into an alienated and class-stratified society. That is, schooling reproduces the social relations of the larger society from generation to generation.

Schooling: A Production Orientation

Again, however, it does *not* follow that schooling finds its predominant function in reproducing the social relations of *consumption per se*. Rather, it is the social relations of *production* which are relevant to the form and function of modern schooling.

A production orientation to understanding education in the United States can be summarized by what we have called the Correspondence Principle, the educational system functioning not so much through the content of day-to-day activities as the structure of its social relations.[13] There is a close correspondence between the social relations which govern personal interaction in the economy and the social relations of the educational system. Specifically, the relations of authority and control between administrators and teachers, teachers and students, students and students, and students and their work replicate class relations and the hierarchical division of labor. Power is organized along vertical lines of authority from administration to faculty to student body; students have a degree of control over their activities comparable to that of workers. Moreover, the relations of dominance and subordination in education differ by level. The rule-orientation of the high school reflects the close supervision of low-level workers; the internalization of norms and freedom from continual supervision in colleges reflect the social relations of middle-level white-collar work. Junior and community colleges, which fall between, conform to the behavior requisites of dependent technical and supervisory personnel.

A production orientation to the analysis of schooling—that the "hidden curriculum" in mass education reproduces the social relations of production—is reinforced in several distinct bodies of current educational research. First, economists

---

[12] The literature on this subject is immense. Illich himself is quite persuasive, but see also Charles E. Silberman, *Crisis in the Classroom* (New York: Random House, 1970), for a more detailed treatment.

[13] This argument is expanded and documented in Bowles and Gintis, *Schooling in Capitalist America*.

have shown that education, in its role of providing a properly trained labor force, takes its place alongside capital accumulation and technological change as a major source of economic growth.[14] Level of educational attainment is the major non-ascriptive variable in furthering the economic position of individuals.

Second, research shows that the type of personal development produced through schooling and relevant to the individual's productivity as a worker in a capitalist enterprise is primarily *non-cognitive*. That is, profit-maximizing firms find it remunerative to hire more highly educated workers at higher pay, essentially *irrespective* of differences among individuals in cognitive abilities or attainments.[15] In other words, two individuals (white American males) with identical cognitive achievements (intelligence or intellectual attainment) but differing educational levels will not command, on the average, the same income or occupational status. Rather, the economic success of each will correspond closely to the average for his educational level. All individuals with the same level of educational attainment tend to have the same expected mean economic success (racial and sexual discrimination aside). This is not to say that cognitive skills are not necessary to job adequacy in a technological society. Rather, these skills either exist in such profusion (through schooling) or are so easily developed on the job that they are not a criterion for hiring. Nor does this mean that there is no correlation between cognitive attainments (e.g., IQ) and occupational status. Such a correlation exists (although it is quite loose),[16] but is almost totally mediated by formal schooling: the educational system discriminates in favor of the more intelligent, although its contribution to worker productivity does not operate primarily *via* cognitive development.[17]

Thus the education-related worker attributes that employers willingly pay for must be predominantly *affective* characteristics—personality traits, attitudes, modes of self-presentation and motivation. How affective traits that are rewarded in schools come to correspond to the needs of alienated production is revealed by direct inspection of the social relations of the classroom. First, students are rewarded in terms of grades for exhibiting the personality characteristics of good workers

---

[14] See Edward F. Denison, *The Sources of Economic Growth in the United States and the Alternatives Before Us* (New York: Committee for Economic Development, 1962) and Theodore Schultz, *The Economic Value of Education* (New York: Columbia University Press, 1963).

[15] This surprising result is developed in Gintis, "Education, Technology, and the Characteristics of Worker Productivity," *American Economic Review*, 61 (May 1971), 266-279, and is based on a wide variety of statistical data. It is validated and extended by Christopher Jencks et al., *Inequality: A Reassessment of the Effect of Family and Schooling in America* (New York: Basic Books, 1972).

[16] See, e.g., Jencks *et al.*

[17] For more extensive treatment, see Jencks *et al.* and Gintis, "Education, Technology, and the Characteristics of Worker Productivity."

A Radical Critique of Ivan Illich
HERBERT GINTIS

in bureaucratic work roles—proper subordination in relation to authority and the primacy of cognitive as opposed to affective and creative modes of social response—above and beyond any actual effect they may have on cognitive achievement.[18] Second, the hierarchical structure of schooling itself mirrors the social relations of industrial production: students cede control over their learning activities to teachers in the classroom. Just as workers are alienated from both the *process* and the *product* of their work activities, and must be motivated by the external reward of pay and hierarchical status, so the student learns to operate efficiently through the external reward of grades and promotion, effectively alienated from the process of education (learning) and its product (knowledge). Just as the work process is stratified, and workers on different levels in the hierarchy of authority and status are required to display substantively distinct patterns of values, aspirations, personality traits, and modes of "social presentation" (dress, manner of speech, personal identification, and loyalties to a particular social stratum),[19] so the school system stratifies, tracks, and structures social interaction according to criteria of social class and relative scholastic success.[20] The most effectively indoctrinated students are the most valuable to the economic enterprise or state bureaucracy, and also the most successfully integrated into a particular stratum within the hierarchical educational process.[21]

Third, a large body of historical research indicates that the system of mass, formal, and compulsory education arose more or less directly out of changes in productive relations associated with the Industrial Revolution, in its role of supplying a properly socialized and stratified labor force.[22]

[18] For an analysis of relevant data and an extensive bibliography, see Bowles and Gintis, *Schooling in Capitalist America.*

[19] This phenomenon is analyzed in Claus Offe, *Leistungsprinzip und Industrielle Arbeit* (Frankfurt: Europaïsche Verlaganstalt, 1970).

[20] See Merle Curti, *The Social Ideas of American Eductors* (Chicago: Charles Scribner's, 1935); Gintis, "Contre-culture et militantisme politique," *Les Temps Modernes*, 28 année, No. 295 (Feb. 1971), 117-148; André Gorz, "Capitalist Relations of Production and the Socially Necessary Labor Force," in *All We Are Saying . . .* , ed. Arthur Lothstein (New York: G.P. Putnam's, 1970); and Gorz, "Technique, techniciens, et lutte de classes," *Les Temps Modernes*, 28 année, No. 289 (Août-Sept. 1971), 141-180; Samuel Bowles, "Unequal Education and the Reproduction of the Social Division of Labor," in *The Capitalist System,* ed. Edwards, Reich, and Weisskopf; and Bowles, "Contradictions de L'enseignement supérieure," *Les Temps Modernes*, 28 année, No. 301-302 (Août-Sept. 1971), 198-240; and David Bruck, "The Schools of Lowell," unpublished honors thesis, Harvard University, 1971.

[21] This statement is supported by the statistical results of Richard C. Edwards, "Alienation and Inequality: Capitalist Relations of Production in Bureaucratic Enterprises," Diss., Harvard University, 1972.

[22] Michael B. Katz, *The Irony of Early School Reform* (Cambridge, Mass.: Harvard University

The critical turning points in the history of American education have coincided with the perceived failure of the school system to fulfill its functional role in reproducing a properly socialized and stratified labor force, in the face of important qualitative or quantitative changes in the social relations of production. In these periods (e.g., the emergence of the common school system) numerous options were open and openly discussed.[23] The conflict of economic interests eventually culminated in the functional reorientation of the educational system to new labor needs of an altered capitalism.

In the mid- to late 19th century, this took the form of the economy's need to generate a labor force compatible with the factory system from a predominantly agricultural populace. Later, the crisis in education corresponded to the economy's need to import peasant European labor whose social relations of production and derivative culture were incompatible with industrial wage-labor. The resolution of this crisis was a hierarchical, centralized school system corresponding to the ascendance of corporate production. This resolution was not without its own contradictions. It is at this time that the modern school became the focus of tensions between work and play, between the culture of school and the culture of immigrant children, and between the notion of meritocracy and equality. Thus while Illich can *describe* the characteristics of contemporary education, his consumption orientation prevents him from understanding how the system came to be.

Toward a Politics of Education

It seems clear that schools instill the values of docility, degrees of subordination corresponding to different levels in the hierarchy of production, and motivation according to external reward. It seems also true that they do not reward, but instead penalize, creative, self-initiated, cognitively flexible behavior. By inhibiting the full development of individual capacities for meaningful individual activity,

---

Press, 1968); Katz, "From Voluntarism to Bureaucracy in American Education," *Sociology of Education*, 44 (Summer 1971), 297-332; Lawrence Cremin, *The Transformation of the School* (New York: Alfred A. Knopf, 1964); Raymond E. Callahan, *Education and the Cult of Efficiency* (Chicago: University of Chicago Press, 1962); Curti, *The Social Ideas of American Educators*; Bowles, "Unequal Education and the Reproduction of the Social Division of Labor"; Joel Spring, "Education and Progressivism," *History of Education Quarterly*, 10 (Spring 1970), 53-71; David K. Cohen and Marvin Lazerson, "Education and the Corporate Order," *Socialist Revolution*, 3 (March-April 1972), 47-72.

[23] See David B. Tyack, *Turning Points in American Educational History* (Boston: Ginn, 1967); Katz, *The Irony of Early School Reform*; and Katz, "From Voluntarism to Bureaucracy in American Education."

schools produce Illich's contended outcomes: the individual as passive receptor replaces the individual as active agent. But the articulation with the larger society is *production* rather than *consumption*.

If the sources of social problems lay in consumer manipulation of which schooling is both an exemplary instance and a crucial preparation for future manipulation, then a political movement for deschooling might be, as Illich says, "at the root of any movement for human liberation." But if schooling is both itself an *activity context* and preparation for the more important activity context of work then personal consciousness arises not from the elimination of outside manipulation, but from the experience of solidarity and struggles in remolding a mode of social existence. Such consciousness represents not a "return" to the self (essential human nature) but a *restructuring* of the self through new modes of social participation.

Of course this evaluation need not be unidirectional from work to education. Indeed, one of the fundamental bases for assessing the value of an alternative structure of control in production is its compatibility with intrinsically desirable individual development through education. In so far as Illich's left-convivial concept is desirable in any ultimate sense, a reorganization of production should be sought conformable to it. This might involve the development of a vital craft/artistic/technical/service sector in production organized along master-apprentice or group-control lines open to *all* individuals. The development of unalienated work technologies might then articulate harmoniously with learning-web forms in the sphere of education.

But a reorganization of production has other goals as well. For example, any foreseeable future involves a good deal of socially necessary and on balance personally unrewarding labor. However this work may be reorganized, its accomplishment must be based on individual values, attitudes, personality traits, and patterns of motivation adequate to its execution. If equality in social participation is a "revolutionary ideal," this dictates that all contribute equally toward the staffing of the socially necessary work roles. This is possible only if the hierarchical (as opposed to social) division of labor is abolished in favor of the solidary cooperation and participation of workers in control of production. Illich's anarchistic notion of learning webs does not seem conducive to the development of personal characteristics for this type of social solidarity.[24]

---

[24] The main elements in Illich's left-convivial "learning web" alternative to manipulative education are all fundamentally dispersive and fragmenting of a learning community:

1. Reference Services to Educational Objects—which facilitate access to things or processes used for formal learning. Some of these things can be reserved for this purpose, stored in li-

These considerations illustrate the shortcomings of Illich's approach to specifying educational structure even in the most ideal of social settings: the fully-formed egalitarian and liberating society. Yet at least two additional social settings must be discussed to achieve even a skeletal picture of educational politics. In both cases the Correspondence Principle plays a critical role.

The second setting for a politics of education is the *transitional society*—one which bears the technological and cultural heritage of the capitalist class/caste system, but whose social institutions and patterns of social consciousness are geared toward the progressive realization of "ideal forms" (i.e., revolutionary goals). In this setting, the social relations of education will themselves be transitional in nature, mirroring the transformation process of social relations of production.[25] For instance, the elimination of boring, unhealthy, fragmented, uncreative, constraining, and otherwise alienated but socially necessary labor requires an extended process of technological change in a transitional phase. As we have observed, the repressive application of technology toward the formation of occupational roles is not due to the intrinsic nature of physical science nor to the requisites of productive efficiency, but to the political imperative of stable control from the top in an enterprise. Nevertheless the shift to automated, decentralized, and worker-controlled technologies requires the continuous supervision and cooperation of workers themselves. Any form this takes in a transitional society will include a constant struggle among three groups: managers concerned with the development of the enterprise, technicians concerned with the scientific rationality of production, and workers concerned with the impact of innovation and management on job satisfaction.[26]

---

braries, rental agencies, laboratories, and showrooms like museums and theaters; others can be in daily use in factories, airports, or on farms, but made available to students as apprentices or on off-hours.

2. Skill Exchanges—which permit persons to list their skills, the conditions under which they are willing to serve as models for others who want to learn these skills, and the addresses at which they can be reached.

3. Peer-Matching—a communications network which permits persons to describe the learning activity in which they wish to engage, in the hope of finding a partner for the inquiry.

4. Reference Services to Educators-at-Large—who can be listed in a directory giving the addresses and self-descriptions of professionals, paraprofessionals, and free-lancers, along with conditions of access to their services.

[25] Samuel Bowles, "Cuban Education and the Revolutionary Ideology," *Harvard Educational Review*, 41 (November 1971), 472-500.

[26] Marco Maccio, "Parti, technicien et classe ouvrière dans la Revolution Chinoise," *Les Temps Modernes*, 27 année, No. 289-290 (Août-Sept. 1970), 215-241; and Gorz, "Techniques, techniciens et lutte de classes."

A Radical Critique of Ivan Illich
HERBERT GINTIS

The present educational system does not develop in the individual the capacities for cooperation, struggle, autonomy, and judgment appropriate to this task. But neither does Illich's alternative which avoids the affective aspects of work socialization totally, and takes technology out of the heads of learners.

In a transitional setting, liberating technologies cannot arise in education, any more than in production, spontaneously or by imposition from above. The social relations of unalienated education must evolve from conscious cooperation and struggle among educational administrators (managers), teachers (technicians), and students (workers), although admittedly in a context of radically redistributed power among the three. The outcome of such a struggle is not only the positive development of education but the fostering of work-capacities in individuals adequate to the task of social transition in work and community life as well.[27]

The inadequacy of Illich's conception of education in transitional societies is striking in his treatment of China and Cuba. It is quite evident that these countries are following new and historically unprecedented directions of social development. But Illich argues the necessity of their failure from the simple fact that they have not deschooled. That they were essentially "deschooled" *before* the revolution (with no appreciable social benefits) does not faze him. While we may welcome and embrace Illich's emphasis on the social relations of education as a crucial variable in their internal development toward new social forms, his own criterion is without practical application.

The third setting in which the politics of education must be assessed—and the one which would most closely represent the American reality—is that of capitalist society itself. Here the correspondence principle implies that educational reform requires an *internal failure* in the stable reproduction of the economic relations of production. That is, the idea of liberating education does not arise spontaneously, but is made possible by emerging contradictions in the larger society. Nor does its aim succeed or fail according as its ethical value is greater or less. Rather, success of the aim presupposes a correct understanding of its basis in the con-

---

[27] The theory of political organization which takes *contradictions* among the interests of the various groups participating in the control of a social activity context as central to social development, underlies my argument. This theory is well developed in Chinese Communist thought, as presented in Mao Tse-tung, "On Contradiction" in *Selected Works* (Peking: Foreign Language Press, 1952), and Franz Schurmann, *Ideology and Organization in Communist China* (Berkeley: University of California Press, 1970). In terms of this "dialectical theory of political action," the reorganization of power in education in a transitional society must render the contradictions among administrators, teachers, and students *non-antagonistic*, in the sense that the day-to-day outcomes of their struggles are the positive, healthy development of the educational system, beneficial to all parties concerned.

traditions in social life, and the political strategies adopted as the basis of this understanding.

The immediate strategies of a movement for educational reform, then, are political: a) understanding the concrete contradictions in economic life and the way they are reflected in the educational system; b) fighting to insure that consciousness of these contradictions persists by thwarting attempts of ruling elites to attenuate them by co-optation; and c) using the persistence of contradictions in society at large to expand the political base and power of a revolutionary movement, that is, a movement for educational reform must understand the social conditions of its emergence and development in the concrete conditions of social life. Unless we achieve such an understanding and use it as the basis of political *action*, a functional reorientation will occur vis-a-vis the present crisis in education, as it did in earlier critical moments in the history of American education.

In the present period, the relevant contradiction involves: a) Blacks moved from rural independent agriculture and seasonal farm wage-labor to the urban-industrial wage-labor system; b) middle-class youth with values attuned to economic participation as entrepreneurs, elite white-collar and professional and technical labor, faced with the elimination of entrepreneurship, the corporatization of production, and the proletarianization of white-collar work[28]; and c) women, the major sufferers of ascriptive discrimination in production (including household production) in an era where capitalist relations of production are increasingly legitimized by their sole reliance on achievement (non-ascriptive) norms.[29]

This inventory is partial, incomplete, and insufficiently analyzed. But only on a basis of its completion can a successful educational strategy be forged. In the realm of contradictions, the correspondence principle must yet provide the method of analysis and action. We must assess political strategies in education on the basis of the single—but distressingly complex—question: will they lead to the transitional society?

I have already argued that deschooling will inevitably lead to a situation of social chaos, but probably not to a serious mass movement toward constructive social change. In this case the correspondence principle simply fails to hold, producing at best a temporary (in case the ruling elites can find an alternative mode of worker socialization) or ultimately fatal (in case they cannot) breakdown in the

[28] Bowles and Gintis, *Schooling in Capitalist America*.
[29] For a general discussion of these issues, see Edwards, Reich, and Weisskopf, ed., *The Capitalist System*.

A Radical Critique of Ivan Illich
HERBERT GINTIS

social fabric. But only if we posit some essential pre-social human nature on which individuals draw when normal paths of individual development are abolished, might this lead in itself to liberating alternatives.

But the argument over the sufficiency of deschooling is nearly irrelevant. For schools are so important to the reproduction of capitalist society that they are unlikely to crumble under any but the most massive political onslaughts. "Each of us," says Illich, "is personally responsible for his or her own de-schooling, and only we have the power to do it." This is not true. Schooling is legally *obligatory*, and is the *major means of access* to welfare-relevant activity contexts. The political consciousness behind a frontal attack on institutionalized education would necessarily spill over to attacks on other major institutions. "The risks of a revolt against school," says Illich,

... are unforeseeable, but they are not as horrible as those of a revolution starting in any other major institution. School is not yet organized for self-protection as effectively as a nation-state, or even a large corporation. Liberation from the grip of schools could be bloodless. *(DS, p. 49)*

This is no more than whistling in the dark.

The only presently viable political strategy in education—and the precise *negation* of Illich's recommendations—is what Rudi Deutchke terms "the long march through the institutions," involving localized struggles for what André Gorz calls "non-reformist reforms," i.e., reforms which effectively strengthen the power of teachers vis-a-vis administrators, and of students vis-a-vis teachers.

Still, although schools neither can nor should be eliminated, the social relations of education *can* be altered through genuine struggle. Moreover, the experience of both struggle and control prepares the student for a future of political activity in factory and office.

In other words, the correct immediate political goal is the nurturing of individuals both liberated (i.e., demanding control over their lives and outlets for their creative activities and relationships) *and* politically aware of the true nature of their misalignment with the larger society. There may indeed be a bloodless solution to the problem of revolution, but certainly none more simple than this.

Conclusion

Illich recognizes that the problems of advanced industrial societies are institutional, and that their solutions lie deep in the social core. Therefore, he consciously rejects a partial or affirmative analysis which would accept society's dominant ideological forms and direct its innovative contributions toward marginal changes in assumptions and boundary conditions.

Instead, he employs a methodology of total critique and negation, and his successes, such as they are, stem from that choice. Ultimately, however, his analysis is incomplete.

Dialectical analysis begins with society as is (thesis), entertains its negation (antithesis), and *overcomes* both in a radical reconceptualization (synthesis). Negation is a form of demystification—a drawing away from the immediately given by viewing it as a "negative totality." But negation is not without presuppositions, is not itself a form of liberation. It cannot "wipe clean the slate" of ideological representation of the world or one's objective position in it. The son/daughter who acts on the negation of parental and societal values is not free—he/she is merely the constrained negative image of that which he/she rejects (e.g., the negation of work, consumption order, and rationality is not liberation but negative un-freedom). The negation of male dominance is not women's liberation but the (negative) affirmation of "female masculinity." Women's liberation in dialectical terms can be conceived of as the overcoming (synthesis) of male dominance (thesis) and female masculinity (antithesis) in a new totality which rejects/embodies both. It is this act of overcoming (synthesis, consciousness) which is the critical and liberating aspect of dialectical thought. Action lies not in the act of negation (antithesis, demystification) but in the act of overcoming (synthesis/consciousness).

The strengths of Illich's analysis lie in his consistent and pervasive methodology of negation. The essential elements in the liberal conceptions of the Good Life—consumption and education, the welfare state and corporate manipulation—are demystified and laid bare in the light of critical, negative thought. Illich's failures can be consistently traced to his refusal to pass *beyond* negations—beyond a total rejection of the appearances of life in advanced industrial societies—to a higher synthesis. While Illich should not be criticized for failing to *achieve* such a synthesis, nevertheless he must be taken seriously to task for mystifying the nature of his own contribution and refusing to step—however tentatively—beyond it. Work is alienating—Illich rejects work; consumption is unfulfilling—Illich rejects consumption; institutions are manipulative—Illich places "nonaddictiveness" at the center of his conception of human institutions; production is bureaucratic—Illich glorifies the entrepreneurial and small-scale enterprise; schools are dehumanizing—Illich rejects schools; political life is oppressive and ideologically totalitarian—Illich rejects politics in favor of individual liberation. Only in one sphere does he go beyond negation, and this defines his major contribution. While technology is in fact dehumanizing (thesis), he does *not* reject technology (antithesis). Rather he goes beyond technology *and* its negation towards a schema of liberating technological forms in education.

The cost of his failure to pass beyond negation in the sphere of social relations in general, curiously enough, is an implicit affirmation of the deepest characteristics of the existing order.[30] In rejecting work, Illich affirms that it *necessarily* is alienating—reinforcing a fundamental pessimism on which the acceptance of capitalism is based; in rejecting consumption, he affirms either that it is inherently unfulfilling (the Protestant ethic), or would be fulfilling if unmanipulated; in rejecting manipulative and bureaucratic "delivery systems," he affirms the *laissez-faire* capitalist model and its core institutions; in rejecting schools, Illich embraces a commodity-fetishist cafeteria-smorgasbord ideal in education; and in rejecting political action, he affirms a utilitarian individualistic conception of humanity. In all cases, Illich's analysis fails to pass beyond the given (in both its positive and negative totalities), and hence affirms it.

The most serious lapse in Illich's analysis is his implicit postulation of a human "essence" in all of us, preceding all social experience—potentially blossoming but repressed by manipulative institutions. Indeed, Illich is logically compelled to accept such a conception by the very nature of his methodology of negation. The given is capitalist (or state socialist) socialization—repressive and dehumanizing. The antithesis is no socialization at all—individuals seeking independently and detached from any mode of social integration their personal paths of development. Such a view of personal growth becomes meaningful in human terms only when anchored in some absolute human standard within the individual and anterior to the social experience that it generates.

In such a conception of individual "essence," critical judgment enters, I have emphasized, precisely at the level of sensing and interpreting one's pre-social psyche. This ability requires only demystification (negation); hence a methodology of negation is raised to a sufficient condition of a liberating social science. Dialectical analysis, on the other hand, takes negation (demystification) as the major *precondition* of liberation, but not its sufficient condition. Even the most liberating historical periods (e.g., the Reformation, the French and American Revolutions), despite their florid and passionately idealistic rhetoric, in fact responded to histori-

---

[30] Indeed to stop one's analysis at negation normally leads to implicit affirmation. For a discussion of this, see "The Affirmative Character of Culture," in Herbert Marcuse, *Negations* (Boston: Beacon Press, 1968).

cally specific potentials and to limited but crucial facets of human deprivation. Dialectical analysis would view our present situation as analogous and, rejecting "human essence" as a pre-social driving force in social change, would see the central struggles of our era as specific negations *and their overcoming* in localizable areas of human concern—while embracing the ideologies that support these struggles.

The place of critical judgment (reason) in this analysis model lies in a realistic-visionary annihilation of both existing society *and* its negation-in-thought in a new, yet historically limited, synthesis. I have argued that this task requires as its point of departure the core economic institutions regulating social life—first in coming to understand their operation and the way in which they produce the outcomes of alienating work, fragmented community, environmental destruction, commodity fetishism, and other estranged cultural forms (thesis), and then in entertaining how we might negate and overcome them through political action and personal consciousness. Illich, in his next book, might leave the security and comfort of negation, and apply his creative vitality to this most demanding of tasks.

An Ethical Model for the Study of Values

DENIS GOULET

Center for the Study of Development and Social Change

The author challenges conventional notions of societal development as dynamic economic performance, modernization of institutions or proliferation of goods and services. For him, authentic development aims toward the realization of human capabilities in all spheres. He examines common assumptions of social scientists who study value change in non-technological societies, contrasting these with another view on the dynamics of value change. Dr. Goulet presents an alternative research model which requires researchers to make themselves vulnerable to the populace under study.

Development is above all a question of values.[1] It involves human attitudes and preferences, self-defined goals, and criteria for determining what are tolerable costs to be borne in the course of change. These are far more important than better resource allocation, upgraded skills, or the rationalization of administrative procedures. Moreover, developmental processes themselves are dialectical,

Copyright © 1971, Denis Goulet

[1] In common discourse, "values" refer in a general way to attitudes, preferences, life-styles, normative frameworks, symbolic universes, belief systems, and networks of meaning men give to life. Sociologists, psychologists, philosophers, and others have always had great difficulty in defining the term with precision. I shall not attempt in these pages to review or assess the extensive literature on values. But for purposes of clarity, it may help the reader to know that I define a "value" as any object or representation which can be perceived by a subject as habitually worthy of desire.

fraught with contradictions, conflicts, and unpredictable reversals of prior trends. At its most profound level, development is an ambiguous historical adventure born of tensions between *what* is sought and *how* it is obtained. When technological innovations or novel behavior patterns impinge on societies living in relative equilibrium, their values are deeply troubled. This is so because such innovations create new strains between demands and effective ability to meet them. Expanded demands may bear on information, material goods, services, freedom, or other presumed benefits. Yet all such changes, usually proposed under the banner of "development," can threaten the very survival of a society's deepest values. Notwithstanding this danger, the dynamics of value change remain poorly understood by development scholars and little respected by agents of change.

Educators, researchers, and planners are conspicuously engaged in the transfer of technologies, not the least of which are research techniques. Moreover, value crises in under-developed societies are closely linked to those faced by industrialized nations such as the United States. For these reasons alone, it is essential to engage in critical inquiry into the value assumptions underlying research.

Ethical judgments regarding the good life, the good society, and the quality of relations among men always serve, directly or indirectly, as operational criteria for development planners and as guidelines for researchers. The main premise of this essay is that conventional social science research on values is deficient because it is incapable of treating values other than instrumentally. It views the values of a populace either as aids or as obstacles to achieving development, which itself is uncritically assumed to be good. The result is that values are subordinated to the goals of development. Yet it is this very equation that must be inverted, for development itself is but an instrumental good. What is conventionally termed development—dynamic economic performance, modern institutions, the availability of abundant goods and services—is simply one possibility, among many, of development in a broader, more critical sense. Authentic development aims at the full realization of human capabilities: men and women become makers of their own histories, personal and societal. They free themselves from every servitude imposed by nature or by oppressive systems, they achieve wisdom in their mastery over nature and over their own wants, they create new webs of solidarity based not on domination but on reciprocity among themselves, they achieve a

---

I take this occasion to thank Marco Walshok for many stimulating exchanges on values over the years 1966 through 1968.

The Study of Values
DENIS GOULET

rich symbiosis between contemplation and transforming action, between efficiency and free expression. This total concept of development can perhaps best be expressed as the "human ascent"—the ascent of all men in their integral humanity, including the economic, biological, psychological, social, cultural, ideological, spiritual, mystical, and transcendental dimensions.

It follows from this view of authentic development that innovation can be good only if it is judged by the concerned populace to be compatible with its image of the good life and the good society. *This is why open, popular debate on values must precede significant impingements, including the interference wrought by research itself, upon a society's life. Both planners, who seek to design strategies for inducing change, and researchers, who profess merely to study change, must submit their assumptions to careful public scrutiny.*

This essay will explore requirements for an ethically acceptable model of research on values, by contrasting the value assumptions of social scientists with another viewpoint on the dynamics of value change and by sketching out an alternative research model based on the pioneering work of French change theorist Georges Allo.

The Dynamics of Value Change

Assumptions of Western Social Scientists

Most social scientists studying change readily assume development to be good or, at least, inevitable. Implicitly or explicitly, they are inclined to believe that modern societies offer greater possibilities for more individuals than non-modern ones. More specifically, they assume that lives governed by a secular world view are more rewarding than those based on a sacred outlook, that technological rationality, division of labor, merit systems, and achievement orientation are superior to their opposites: organic symbolism, undifferentiated functions, ascription reward systems, and motivations founded upon cooperation and constraints upon desire. Underlying these assumptions is the conviction that a rational quest for knowledge should supplant the quest oriented toward initiation to a sense of mystery and wisdom. Spokesmen for the Third World's emerging consciousness, however, reject this view as ethnocentric and disdainful of all human values not amenable to rational treatment.

Social science, thanks to its positivist bias, favors quantity over quality. It processes qualities with quantitative instruments of measurement and classification, thereby losing that precise element which makes them more than mere quantity. It is true that quantitative changes of a sufficient magnitude may produce changes in quality, but even in these cases, the uniquely qualitative dimensions of reality tend to escape the purview of those best equipped to measure or describe quantitative facets of a whole. Consequently, one may reasonably doubt the ability of social scientists to perceive qualitative manifestations of value change except through the distorting lens of their own positivist bias. Especially in the case of values, the "object" studied has no intelligibility apart from its "subjective" resonances. Moreover, the quantitative bias inherent in empirical science imperceptibly blends into a second bias, reductionism, which grants primacy to a theoretical framework of hypotheses over the totality of experience. Values belong to realms of synthesis, not analysis: their proper domains are philosophy, poetry, meta-analytical symbolism. Only under stringent conditions to be discussed later in this essay is the study of values appropriate to social science. To reduce this synthesis of totality to that mere portion of reality which is measurable is to deprive life of its specificity and to falsify reality itself.

There is no need here to deal at length with the consequences of a third bias of social scientists, elitism. Researchers practice a new form of clericalism—not of ordained clerks, but of methodologists initiated to the exclusive task of explaining reality's crucial dimensions. No matter how insistently an individual researcher disclaims elitist views, he is in fact the possessor of a mysterious tool-kit the contents of which cannot be fathomed by the "objects" of his study. The stance of the researcher manifests something of the "magical" posture described by Levi-Strauss when he speaks of the power which accrues to anthropologists investigating primitives who lack mastery over the written word.

The most damaging value bias held by emphirical researchers is the belief that all social realities are amendable to "objective" study. But Clyde Kluckhohn and others report, significantly, "that when one studies values directly, the values are changed by the processes of study itself . . . Thus the mere focusing of attention upon value-problems changes the problems. In so far as this hypothesis is correct, the values we discover are in part a function of the research approach."[2]

My contention goes further: that problems are changed even when values are studied *indirectly*. The mere presence of researchers on values among people

---

[2] Clyde Kluckhohn *et al.*, "Values and Value-Orientations in the Theory of Action," in *Toward a General Theory of Action*, ed. Talcott Parsons and Edward A. Shils (New York: Harper Torchbooks, 1962), p. 408.

alters their level of consciousness regarding those values. Wittingly or unwittingly, researchers are vectors of certain images of the good life and the good society; their passage does not leave the values of a populace untouched.

Of course, the field investigators have long practiced the art of participant observation, but participation is subordinated to observation and to the demands of research. This stance proves especially inadequate in cases where existential immersion is indispensable to gain understanding of the motivational dynamics at work in societies. For example, one can never capture the spiritual meaning of Zen by merely observing the routine of a Zen monastery. Instead, one must "let go" intellectually and suspend the ordinary canons of rational judgment. And so with the student of guerrilla movements; in moments of crisis he cannot maintain his observer's role because to refrain from action is to impede the success of that action.[3]

The practical lesson to be drawn here is that the investigator should make himself vulnerable in the conduct of his research. Yet most researchers are uncomfortable when the demands of participation interfere with those of observation. This predisposition poses a major stumbling-block to the valid study of values in changing societies. Furthermore, even when a research sponsor's credentials are untainted, the special knowledge a researcher possesses can intimidate people.

These difficulties are compounded by the tendency of value researchers to describe their activity as one carried out *in the study mode,* whereas in truth it is a special kind of interference *in the action mode:* the long term impact of their research is to prepare the way for subsequent efforts by others to induce value changes among fragile populations. Such research, ignorant of the true dynamics of value change, inevitably leads to the manipulation of people. Only by restructuring the research enterprise can manipulation be avoided: "objects" of study must become "subjects" actively defining the ground-rules by which their values are studied. No researcher can afford to ignore the dynamics of value change and its practical implications for his own vulnerability *vis-a-vis* the populace he studies.

The Crisis in Values and the Concept of Existence Rationality

What happens to values in a non-technological society when important changes

---

[3] This statement is based on discussions with Colombian sociologist Orlando Fals Borda, author of *Subversion and Social Change in Colombia* (New York: Columbia Univ. Press, 1969).

are proposed to it or imposed upon it? The key to understanding such a process is the concept of "existence rationality." Before analyzing this concept, however, my assumptions about the relationship between values and change must be stated explicitly. These assumptions are as follows:

1. In non-developed societies, a close nexus exists between normative and significative values.[4] "What ought to be done" in any domain—family relations, work, commercial exchange, dealing with leaders—is intimately related to the symbols society uses to explain the meaning of life and death.

2. In developed societies, on the other hand, no such nexus exists and no unifying vision of life's total meaning is shared. On the contrary, great tolerance is exhibited toward a variety of significative values. A Mormon businessman, for example, can behave professionally in quite the same way as his agnostic counterpart. Their norms may be the same, but not the significance of those norms for each of them.

Although "underdeveloped" societies are characterized by a high level integration among diverse values, their economies are fragmented. The opposite condition prevails in developed areas: symbols are not linked to norms, but economic activity is so highly integrated that subsistence autarchy becomes practically impossible.

The importance of the nexus between norms and meaning lies in this: that in traditional societies work is a cosmic act, while in developed societies it is a specialized function.

3. Traditional societies receive stimuli to change which clearly challenge their prevailing *normative values*. These stimuli present different ways of doing things: planting crops, educating children, or practicing hygiene. More fundamentally they introduce new objectives to human effort: to improve one's level of living, to obtain a "better" house or more food, to gain greater mobility so as to work and travel elsewhere.

---

[4] Norms refer to rules of action; signification is explanatory and/or symbolic. Although detailed exegesis of this terminology lies beyond the scope of the present essay, a brief explanation of the difference between the two categories of values may prove helpful.

Values can be classified according to several criteria: content, mode of perception, and so on. The distinction between normative and significative values is based on diverse modes of perception. Thus values can be perceived as operative or as significative.

"Operative" values deal with objects or representations "worthy of acting upon." But this does not mean that every operative value is necessarily normative. A given subject may judge that his total situation exempts him from the duty of acting according to an operative value. He may also conclude that such a value is simply a general statement to which he must pay "normative homage." On the other hand, a "norm" is a specific kind of operative value which is perceived by

The Study of Values
DENIS GOULET

4. By challenging extant norms, these stimuli either create or reveal crisis: should the members of society continue to act as before or change their norms and ways?

5. Inasmuch as norms are intimately bound to significative values, these stimuli also threaten that society's entire world of meaning. Traditional norms of behavior are derived from a given universe of explanations. When norms are challenged, that belief system itself is also attacked. I have witnessed, for example, the profound deterioration of a father's authority over his sons during the Algerian war of independence because scarcity of food obliged his sons to take a salaried job on a French road construction gang. The same circumstances also affected his degree of control over his wives because the French government, in an effort to counteract propaganda efforts by the FLN (Algerian National Liberation Front), organized a referendum in 1958 to induce natives to keep the French government in power. Relentless efforts were made to pressure Moslem women to vote in this referendum. Even in the small Sahara town where I lived with two semi-nomadic tribes, the referendum campaign conducted by the French had overwhelming impact on the entire Islamic life-view of the community. Significant stimuli to modify behavioral norms do attack the symbolic system of pre-developed societies. As a result, the nexus between normative and significative values is shattered.

6. Once this nexus is shattered, the affected societies are left with two options, both very unpleasant. The first is to maintain belief in significative values even if these have become incompatible with norms of behavior which increasingly determine day-to-day activity. Such fragmentation is psychologically harmful for men who have been accustomed to see cosmic, if not mystical, meaning even in simple actions carried out in the home, in the field, or on the pathways. Not only is a serious social identity problem posed, but the inducements to new behavior tend to be rejected totally or, in the opposite case, uncritically internalized, often with damaging side-effects. Western development writers are fond of praising "achieve-

---

the subject as directing his actions. This terminology remains ambiguous, however, inasmuch as a subject's self-fulfillment (real or illusory) can always be for him *a* norm enabling him to go against *the* norm (social or moral).

"Significative" values are quite different: they confer meaning and significance to existence. Certain significative values, although not all, are all-embracing. These are what we designate when we speak of a *Weltanschauung*, a belief system, a philosophy of life, a symbolic universe, a network of myths.

There need not always exist a close connection between significative and operative values (of which norms are one kind). Nevertheless, the requirements of vital organization (in a person or within a society) and of minimal intelligibility may rule out certain extreme antinomies, inasmuch as too sharp a split is disruptive of identity, perhaps even of life itself.

ment orientation" and the spirit of initiative. Nevertheless, in many societies (among villagers in India, Gypsies in southern Spain, Indians of the Amazon) achievement orientation is viewed as a moral aberration as reprehensible as theft or criminal neglect in other societies. The first option presented to incipient "transitional" societies is to live in a state of painful cultural fragmentation.

The other choice theoretically open to them is to fashion a new nexus between values which give meaning and those which provide rules for action. From the very nature of the case, however, such synthesis is impossible. How can groups undergoing their first experience with modern technology develop a synthesis of meaning when advanced countries themselves, after almost two centuries of painful initiation to specialized knowledge and technical practices, have proved incapable of formulating a wisdom to match their sciences? Critics in the West correctly denounce the failure of their own societies to provide an intellectually valid framework of broad goals and criteria against which to evaluate the partial accomplishments of science or technique. In Danilo Dolci's words, "We have become experts when it comes to machinery, but we are still novices in dealing with organisms."[5] Non-developed societies lack that familiarity with specialized science and quasi-autonomous technologies which might enable them to make a new nexus or synthesis. Therefore, they have no realistic hope of maintaining unity in their world of values by assimilating of new techniques. They are doomed to social disruption.

Guided by these assumptions, one may search for a strategy of value change dictated by the experience of living communities. One might base such a strategy on *existence rationality,* a concept which suggests a manner of studying values without manipulating those who adhere to them. Existence rationality is the vital process by which all societies, within the limits of their information-processing capacities and other constraints, devise optimum strategies for obtaining their goals. Common to all existence rationalities are two kinds of values: certain core values which constitute the inner limits of that rationality, and others which are its outer boundaries. Inner limits are the indispensable core values and aspirations without which a society loses cohesiveness and its members can no longer identify with the group. Outer boundaries, in turn, are broad zones of attitudes and behavior in which departures from normal social demands are permitted because they do not directly threaten survival, esteem or freedom.

[5] Danilo Dolci, "Mafia-Client Politics," *Saturday Review,* July 6, 1968, p. 51.

The Study of Values
DENIS GOULET

Within all existence rationalities, survival is a minimum objective of social effort. Moreover, every society strives to improve its ability to sustain life, as well as to meet a variety of needs related to esteem and freedom. Otherwise stated, there exist certain minimal demands for survival, identity, solidarity, and dignity. Even those societies called underdeveloped are able to meet these minimum objectives although, it is true, they cannot provide their members with the full range of material satisfactions or with those particular psychological satisfactions which require abundant goods. And if, as I have argued elsewhere,[6] the broad goals of development are *optimum* life-sustenance, esteem, and freedom, it follows that all change pedagogies must aim at restructuring or expanding the outer boundaries of a society's existence rationality, not at eliminating its core values.

Conventional development strategies have not recognized this distinction. Consequently, they are often perceived as a threat to the core values without which a society cannot preserve its identity. Insensitive change strategies do, in fact, pose such a threat. This is why "underdeveloped" societies often *appear* to reject or resist the rationality associated wth developmental innovations, as they continue to struggle for survival in altered circumstances. The burden of my argument is, in short, that no inherent resistance to change can be found in "underdeveloped" societies. What exists is rather an almost instinctive resistance to any attempt to implant change which does not respect the inner limits of the given society's existence rationality.

If "intruder" values, whether introduced overtly or covertly, are to be accepted by members of a society whose existence rationality is of the traditional sort, three conditions must be met:

1. Vital resources hitherto unavailable must become exploitable. This means that old constraints rooted in the paucity of resources or in rigid allocation systems must be loosened.

2. New capacities for handling information must be generated; that is, ways must be found enabling men to process a greater amount and variety of information than before.

3. The alien rationality of modernization must be critically linked, by the people themselves, to their traditional existence rationalities. Above all, the core

---

[6] Cf. Denis A. Goulet, "Development For What?" *Comparative Political Studies*, 1 (July 1968), 295-312; and Goulet, "On the Goals of Development," *Cross Currents*, 28 (Fall 1968), 387-405.

values common to all existence rationalities—survival, basic esteem, and freedom —must be preserved.

Even a narrow existence rationality offers considerable scope for changes, provided these reinforce the dominant strategy the society has adopted to assure life-sustenance, the search for esteem (especially in-group esteem), group fulfillment, and freedom from unwanted determinisms. Even if they are unable to plan a different future for themselves or gain occupational and social mobility, people from underdeveloped societies are able to conceive of freedom in spatial or symbolic terms. This is why change strategies aimed at objectives such as increasing the kinds of mobility associated with modern societies can protect the inner limits of prevailing existence rationalities while simultaneously expanding their outer boundaries. Tangible rewards will be assured to those who remain faithful to the core of their **group's** existence rationality while contributing to its expansion. And rewards will be denied to those who "betray" the group's existence rationality by uncritically adopting a totally alien one, that is, modernization. Native, no less than foreign, modernizers are often uncritical bearers of values hidden behind the screen of visible benefits. However, the critical abilities of change agents themselves are very meager. Consequently, development's alleged beneficiaries need to develop a critical capacity themselves before their destiny is decided in accord with unexamined patterns of modernization. Unless a deliberate strategy counteracts present trends, most transfers will continue to take place uncritically. Too many change strategists prematurely conclude that development is incompatible with "traditional" value systems, and fail to tailor development's potential benefits to traditional existence rationalities.

As circumstances vary, innovation may take the form of highly individualistic entrepreneurship and stress creativity, or it may generate new forms of collaboration. For example, even where economic output appears stationary to economists, some members of the society are able to imagine hypothetical conditions wherein the total product is not stationary. Consequently, there is considerable latitude in the degree to which personally beneficial innovation can be tolerated. Such innovation need not necessarily be viewed as injurious, either to the society's other members or to the group's core values. Indeed, psychic and symbolic mobility may be considerable in traditional societies although less apparent than in transitional or modern societies. It is not "underdeveloped" value structures which are obstacles to change, but rather insensitive impact strategies which snuff out traditional societies' latent potential for change. Where respect for core

The Study of Values
DENIS GOULET

values is maintained, this potential can be kineticized and innovation can be incorporated into old existence rationalities.

The concept of existence rationality outlined here grew out of my field research on values among Gypsies in southern Spain. In this case, as in others, the view that a hostile traditional society would resist change has proven wrong.[7] On the contrary, great potential for change became apparent once the distinction between the inner limits and the outer boundaries of an existence rationality was postulated. Although this hypothesis has not been definitely established, even for Gypsies themselves, it opens new vistas for inducing social change in ways which minimize the destruction of existing value systems.

The Vulnerability of Researchers

Culturally, economically, and politically, underdevelopment is experienced as structural vulnerability.[8] Sound cultural values in many societies are thus susceptible to being destroyed because change agents, rendered incompetent by their ethnocentrism, declare these values to be incompatible with the "modern" values of productivity, efficiency, and impersonal human relations. This global phenomenon occurs within the U.S. educational system itself. White school teachers usually require Black ghetto students to assimilate white middle-class values and standards. Behind seemingly good objectives such as high standards of achievement, competent teaching, remedial programs for youngsters who have fallen behind, and enrichment programs for children who are "culturally deprived," a powerful campaign is waged, at times unconsciously by well-meaning benefactors, to destroy the pride of Blacks in their own cultural accomplishments.

Every society needs to have its values respected if it is to embark on an uncertain future with confidence in its own ability to control that future. All efforts to introduce modernity, efficiency, and technological rationality risk being destructive if change agents uncritically assume these qualities to be superior to those they supplant. Obviously, neither bad hygiene nor superstition ought to

---

[7] Numerous interviews conducted around projective themes suggested by Gypsies themselves revealed willingness to change in all cases in which proposed changes were explicitly related to their own self-expressed "outer margin" values. More importantly, Gypsies themselves, upon exploration, came to conclude that even changes which they initially rejected did not have to be viewed as threatening to their identity or survival. For details, see Denis Goulet and Marco Walshok, "Values Among Underdeveloped Marginals: the Case of Spanish Gypsies," *Comparative Studies in Society and History*, 13, No. 4 (October 1971).

[8] I have discussed structural vulnerability at greater length in *The Cruel Choice* (New York: Atheneum Publishers, 1971), Chapter Two.

be preserved simply because they are picturesque, ancient, or traditional. Any "folkloric" outlook on old values is evidently worthless. On the other hand, Third World societies are now being subjected to the attacks of a technoculture which brands their most cherished self-images as puerile and obsolete. Their vulnerability in the face of "contemporary" cultures is as traumatic for their leaders as for the general populace, inducing in them a deep schizophrenic tension between proud self-affirmation of their own values and rejection of whatever indigenous cultural elements impede modernization. Even more pervasively than in the era of overt colonialism, when the metropole's educational ideals were held out as superior to native ones, today's culture media cast doubt on the worth of all values other than those exported *en masse* by the purveyors of progress. A problem exists because some of the fruits of progress—lower death rates, better food and housing—are genuine benefits. Therefore, the solution is not to reject change but to introduce discernment and creativity in the impact strategies used to stimulate change. Change strategies now in vogue rarely consider the cultural trauma they cause although culture is one of the realms in which the vulnerability of underdeveloped societies is most evident.

We must not suppose that the concept of vulnerability is applicable only to underdeveloped societies. On the contrary, it lies at the heart of the stance adopted by representatives from "advanced" societies in their dealing with others. Experts too are vulnerable: they risk having their technical or methodological superiority held against them unless they ratify their own vulnerability. The crucial question is: are encounters to be founded on reciprocity or on domination? Weaker partners reject domination as invalid, and stronger groups can no longer practice it in good conscience or even with realistic hopes of success. Ultimately, reciprocity is necessary for esteem, an idea which has come of age. And reciprocity is the sole basis for non-manipulative relationships. To achieve reciprocity among societies, however, is as difficult as it is among persons. Serious structural obstacles stand in the way.

Structural paternalism in relationships impedes genuine growth for both partners. What ought to underlie relationships is what Lebret calls "active respect" for others.[9] Passive respect means simply not interfering with the other's growth, whereas active respect enjoins positive action to foster the fulfillment of others on their own terms. Only if the weaker partner in the relationship perceives that

---

[9] L. J. Lebret, *Manifeste Pour Une Civilisation Solidaire* (Paris: Economie et Humanisme, 1959), p. 18.

active respect motivates the other can his internal resentment toward the "helper" be overcome and reciprocity become possible. If the basic experience of underdevelopment is one of vulnerability, developed groups must revise their notion of how to encounter the underdeveloped.

The developed partner can never accurately observe underdevelopment in the detached mode of a spectator. Nor can he properly treat it as a mere problem: he himself is part of the problem. His society is responsible[10] at least for the alteration in the other's aspirations—to achieve dignity and autonomous agency in its own development—even if not for the other's powerlessness to meet these aspirations. Therefore, the relationship can lead to genuine development only if the stronger partner's technical and economic superiority, or the power to impose his cultural values, is somehow neutralized. The mistaken belief that relative superiority is absolute constitutes the principal obstacle to the success of the relationship. Recipients are already vulnerable; donors must become so. Only then can recipients cease being beggars and donors manipulators. In practice, no one can render himself fully vulnerable: but he can expose himself to the other's area of relative superiority and allow the other to make him vulnerable.

Concretely, the technical advisor or researcher from a developed country must somehow experience the other's "underdevelopment" as a radical challenge to the validity of his own "development." He can do this in several ways. First, he can acknowledge to himself that his own superiority is but a relative superiority, attributed to him in virtue of the ethnocentrism dominant in his own society. Second, he can reflect on the powerlessness of his own knowledge and wealth to answer basic value dilemmas posed by the development process. This should at least make him humble about his skills. Third, he can accede to the same kind of critical consciousness of his own values—usually latent in his program, policy, plan, or image of development—that the weaker partner seeks of his own values. *Development and underdevelopment alike are but superficial manifestations of a universal crisis in basic human values*—a crisis bearing on the degree of freedom men can snatch away from the necessitating pressures generated by broad technological processes operative in the world. These processes are as poorly understood, in their totality, by the technologically sophisticated man as by illiterate members of traditional societies. Indeed, developed societies have surrendered themselves to the dynamisms and determinisms of development more totally—

---

[10] On the important difference between responsibility and guilt, see Pierre Antoine, "Qui est coupable?" *Revue de l'Action Populaire*, No. 32 (November 1959), 1055-1065.

perhaps even irrevocably—than those who have just begun to seek development; accordingly, pre-modern societies may hold the key to the solution of post-technological problems faced by groups which embarked on the process of development long ago.

This is the sense in which even "developed" experts are vulnerable, that is, powerless to solve the most fundamental value questions posed by underdevelopment. Once they openly acknowledge their vulnerability, they become able to purge themselves of any sense of superiority in their dealings with underdeveloped counterparts. Indeed, they should concede that the domains wherein their own culture enjoys relative superiority—technique, applied rationality—may be quite insignificant as compared with richer values embodied in the cultures they are facing. There is deep symbolic truth in Lawrence Durrell's belief that our "common actions in reality are simply the sackcloth covering which hides the cloth-of-gold—the meaning of the pattern."[11] It is absurd to compare societies solely on the basis of mere surface performance in economics, politics, or social organization; the inner "meaning" of the patterns is far more significant.

The implications of vulnerability for research can be illustrated by outlining an alternative research model frankly inspired by its author's desire to confer mastery upon the studied populace over its own destiny.

An Alternative Research Model

One approach to the study of values, little known in the United States, is derived from long reflection on experiments in community development, educational planning, and the mobilization of urban and rural populations in several African countries, the Middle East, and Latin America. Its author is Georges Allo,[12] a

[11] Lawrence Durrell, *Justine* (New York: Cardinal Edition, 1957), p. 7.
[12] Georges Allo has described his work in several articles: "Research on Values at the Crossroads of Modern Civilizations," a brochure printed in English and French (Beirut: Institut de Recherche et de Formation En Vue du Développement [IRFED], 1961); "La Recherche de l'IRFED sur les valeurs et les civilisations," *Développement et Civilisations*, No. 13 (March 1963), 104-108; "La Recherche de l'IRFED sur la rencontre moderne des civilisations," *Développement et Civilisations*, No. 14 (June 1963), 113-116; "L'Evolution des valeurs dans une civilisation," *Développement et Civilisations*, No. 20 (December 1964), 78-87; *IRFED VEC (Valeurs et Civilisations) Bulletin de la Recherche*, No. 5 (May 1963) [This text is an evaluation of the 18-month trial run on values research conducted by Allo in the Middle East]; "Revolution des **valeurs**," *Economie et Humanisme*, No. 160 (May/June 1965), 3-10; "Les Valeurs dans la rencontre moderne des civilisation," *Développement et Civilisations*, No. 23 (September 1965), 80-87; "Pourquoi le développement exige un dialogue entre civilisations," *Développement et Civilisations*, No. 34 (June 1968), 61-66; and the entire issue of *Dialogue* (Paris), No. 1 (June 1967), 40 pp.

The Study of Values
DENIS GOULET

French philosopher and change theorist. Allo predicates his values research on a value critique undertaken by the populace itself. His mode of immersion in any field setting combines elements of research, of pedagogy, and of mobilization for change. He views all acceptable value changes—including the heightened consciousness of pre-existing values—as the outcome of dynamic interplay among multiple tensions. The basic premises of Allo's research orientation are as follows:

—all formulations used in studying values need to be made in the language and symbols of those being studied;
—value studies must focus on integrated patterns of total value orientations in a human community;
—total integrated patterns of value cannot be obtained if people are treated as *objects* of observation or interrogation. They must take part in the process of studying their own values as *subjects* or active judges of the study undertaken;
—images and conscious profiles of themselves held by individuals and groups express their values more adequately than descriptions, measurements, correlations, or classifications dealing with their economic activity, political life, kinship structure, or intrasocietal roles;
—while under study, members of developing societies should be allowed to appraise the value changes they are undergoing or which can be anticipated;
—empirical research procedures used by cross-cultural social science disciplines must be allied to modes of reflection which are at once philosophical and phenomenological. This reflection should be conducted jointly by researchers and members of a culture if the distortion produced by fragmentation of value patterns is to be reduced;
—fruitful generalizations about values and scaled needs can only be gained from permanent disciplined exchange among representatives of many value systems in the process of being challenged by modernity.

Allo searches for general conclusions by deliberately confronting diverse value profiles. According to him, comparison and confrontation generate dynamic syntheses of value systems while these undergo evolution. His aim is to focus the attention of researchers on dynamic (not static) value profiles by observing what happens to these profiles when they are challenged by altered conditions. Understanding is gained through a joint effort of "brainstorming" by researchers and participants over how to react, in value terms, to diverse challenges. The knowledge thus obtained can help planners, educators, technicians, and popular leaders appraise the cost, in values, of their own recommendations. More importantly, this approach allows communities to play the decisive role in choosing the speed and direction of their own value change in accord with their preferred images of development. Hence the "pulse-taking" practiced by Allo before social scientists begin to study values reflects his concern to devise a method which eliminates manipulative and elitist biases.

Values as experienced are distorted unless hypotheses and research instruments are derived from a holistic view of these values in their pre-scientific human setting. Scientific fragmentation is inappropriate in this special domain because, by definition, values refer to *evaluational* totality as well as to *valuational* fragments. When he "evaluates," a subject situates his values in an overall framework of standards he deems important. In order to do this, he must posit a reflective act and refer, at least implicitly, to a total pattern of meaning and worthwhileness. When he merely "valuates," on the other hand, a man does not engage in this reflective action nor does he make a critical, or judgmental, reference to his total universe of standards. To "valuate" means simply that he makes a selective preference, to which he joins some judgment about the suitability of the preference and of the object of preference. Since values contain an essentially subjective component, one cannot reduce values to mere objects of study. Any procedure used to study values must respect the complex nature of values as both integral and integrative; one cannot validly examine the values of an individual or society unless he understands the relative position of all that individual's or society's values in their totality. Abstraction and analysis are not thereby ruled out, but they become legitimate only at certain moments in a specified sequence. Indeed, fidelity to this sequence imposes itself as a normative principle. *The goal of a comprehensive research sequence is to achieve permanent evaluative synthesis of dynamic value profiles and to capture the meaning of the evolution of these profiles.* The stages in this process of permanent synthesis are as follows:

1. Preliminary synthesis. The investigator solicits from natural leaders in a community and from popular spokesmen, having no influence beyond their limited kinship or affective circles, their perception of what their total human existential situation is, what it means, and what it ought to be. Information is also obtained as to which changes are affecting them, how society's members assess these changes, what their understanding is of issues lying outside the purview of their daily concerns, and what degree of relevance or interest they impart to these issues. In order to obtain such testimonies, an investigator must obviously engage in intimate and prolonged immersion in the environment studied. More importantly, he must establish relations of confidence with informants. Confidence comprises both trust and the willingness of interlocutors to confide or divulge intimate thoughts. From this phase of "pre-reflection" preceding systematic empirical study, a researcher obtains preliminary global notions of what is valuated and what is evaluated by a populace.

2. Systematic observation. Under ideal conditions, systematic observation should then take place at four different levels. The first is that of primary groups or sub-systems constituting natural units of daily life. General observation can be conducted, for instance, on all aspects of life in a village or among an itinerant tribe. A second level of observation is some limited sector of activity such as work, recreation, worship, or family relations. Third, there is the cultural system as a whole, whether it be the belief system (cognitive values), the set of norms, patterns of interaction, or the total network of social forces affecting cohesion and disruption. A fourth level touches upon the broad world-view, or philosophy of life.

Social science disciplines play a major role in these studies. But, according to Allo, they can be valid only if areas of study are chosen and hypotheses derived from the psychic universe revealed to investigators in the first step of the research sequence, the pre-reflection. This global first approach is the matrix from which empirical research orientations are to flow.

3. Reflective synthesis by the research team. The third stage in the process is the elaboration by the research team of a reflective, critically conscious synthesis, as distinct from the naive synthesis of the first stage. Ideally, the team ought to include members of the society under observation as well as trained investigators from outside. All those who have taken the pulse of the populace in Stage 1 and conducted systematic study at any of the four levels in Stage 2 should confront their findings as a group. The purpose of these sessions is to begin formulating a reflective synthesis of the value universe of the human group under study. This synthesis is not ingenuous or uncritical as it was in Stage 1 since it is formulated at a more explicit level of consciousness than the earlier one. Moreover, it is elaborated only after the investigators themselves have influenced the consciousness of the population. The elements of this new systematization are drawn from findings obtained in prior stages, examined in the light of all available secondary documents and relevant parallel studies. Inasmuch as diverse interest groups, classes, partisans, and ideologies are represented, the resultant reflective value syntheses necessarily vary. Each partial synthesis is made to confront all the others in order to test the critical survival value of each and to probe inductively for possible generality, partial or total.

4. Feedback of reflective synthesis to populace. The final stage of the normative sequence consists in resubmitting the critical syntheses obtained in Stage 3 to the informants who provided the naive synthesis in Stage 1. The choice of appropriate terms and symbols evidently depends on prolonged interaction between the research team and a representative portion of the interested populace. Informants of the initial phase may reject the synthesis elaborated, correct it, or accept it tentatively as a new outlook to be considered in their growing awareness of their own values and value evolution. They may endorse it, with or without qualifications, or they may not understand it.

The research team never arrogates to itself the right to interpret the problems of the native populace, which holds the final veto over the value synthesis elaborated. This synthesis delineates existing value constellations, interprets the significance of challenges posed (or proposed) to these constellations, and explores alternatives in terms of probable futures.

Yet Allo's normative sequence launches a dynamic process of continuous synthesizing among values held, values proposed, and values newly embraced. Underlying the endeavor is Allo's belief that social science can best formulate hypotheses on value change after a pre-reflection, or global approach. The findings of empirical research are then subjected to a treatment which is not abstract or analytical, but critical and "dialogical" in nature. Finally, all knowledge obtained is tested through pedagogical action, which itself leads to mobilization.

Significance of Allo's Method

Allo's method is still embryonic; consequently, one cannot easily pass judgment on its merits. His effort is the by-product of a search to overcome the limitations inherent in empirical methodologies. To empirical study Allo adds three new sources of light: varied experiential testimony, philosophical discourse of a highly critical nature, and the transposition of reflective findings into a language of value synthesis acceptable to interested populaces.

For Allo, dialogue on man is fruitful only when it takes place simultaneously on the positive level of science and on the reflective level of philosophy. He explains his position on the relations between social science and philosophy in these terms:[13]

If dialogue between scientists and philosophers is to be possible and fruitful, all must have attempted to make *a first global approach* to the reality to be studied. This approach is both pre-scientific and pre-philosophic. And it is the same for all. It is an approach which is not specialized but *'existential'* in the sense that one tries to engage in it with everything that he is: intelligence, sensitivity, affective powers, in a word with his entire experience. This experience is no doubt limited: each one's experience is always situated in a given place, it is conditioned and subjective. Nevertheless, it is a first attempt to draw near to a totality and it brands a man with the sense of the whole which he must never lose thereafter. This approach is rich because it is alive. Afterward it is incumbent upon scientific reflection to control all the elements of this totality which lie within its capabilities. Philosophical reflection, in turn, should make a twofold use of findings in its own elaboration: findings seen as a vital whole, and as analyzed by scientific disciplines.

On this common foundation and on all specialized studies undertaken from this point will be built all interdisciplinary work, properly speaking. I see it as *a journey along a common path*. No participant tries to persuade others of the conclusions of his own science or philosophy, but each accepts to retrace in the presence of others the description of his own personal formulation. As they listen to him, others begin to perceive better than before how to relate their viewpoint to that of others; new perceptions enter into play, critiques are formulated. At the end of the road what will have been achieved is a better approach to a human reality which is perennially so complex and so unified. . . . A social scientist who contents himself simply with extracting from my data a few hypotheses he can utilize is disfiguring these data. The reason is that my research formulates its own hypotheses at another level, one which is not immediately transposable into social science research hypotheses. Moreover, to insist on looking first of all for hypotheses is to miss the whole point of the problem, which is *primarily a problem of epistemology*, that is, of critical study of different types of human cognition. All sciences, social sciences like the rest, must first consent to question their own assumptions in terms of a critique of knowledge and of the requirements of action.

For my part, I absolutely refuse to dispense with this sequence of operations, lest I fall into the serious trap of completely bypassing the real problem, namely, the kind of collaboration to be established among all modes of knowing with a view to orienting development in the most human way possible. . . .

---

[13] Allo, in a memorandum to the author, "Réflexions sur notre tentative d'opérer un rapprochement entre la recherche américaine et la recherche de l'IRFED sur le rôle des valeurs dans le développement," (October 25, 1967), 20 pp.

There are, it seems to me, two kinds of biases: a) the bias of a philosophical position which remains latent and unavowed. One must always beware of this and, in effect, science has proved very helpful in this domain by striving after objectivity even before it attempts to explain reality. Philosophy is above all *an interrogation* of reality and, as far as possible, *of total reality*. b) There is also the bias of a scientific hypothesis which runs the risk of interfering surreptitiously with facts and even of distorting them. This is what has frequently taken place with the evolutionary hypothesis as applied to societies. Contemporary anthropologists are not only abandoning this hypothesis but are also denouncing the validity of facts which the hypothesis has often elicited. It is precisely in order to avoid all bias that I advocate the global approach in opposition to all *a prioris*, be they philosophical or scientific.

Science, claims Allo, necessarily fragments reality when it abstracts. He challenges this procedure in the *specific* case of value studies, although not in *general* terms, because by definition values involve evaluational totality, not merely valuational fragments.

Social scientists would surely be guilty of provincialism if, in the name of rigor, they were to limit the use of the term methodology solely to matters of quantitative technique applicable to empirical research situations. As Neil Smelser and others have long contended, methodology in the broad sense governs the larger facets of the scientific enterprise: the logic of theory construction and the derivation of analytic propositions from abstract concepts. It is while deriving propositions from abstract concepts that Allo stretches his reasoning to its logical limits. If the subjective component in *value* is central, he asserts, it follows that values cannot be reduced to mere objects of study. Allo has conducted modest experiments in several continents; it is in the Middle East that he has progressed furthest in beginning to elaborate, with the help of a local team in Lebanon,[14] the outline of a method for achieving permanent synthesis in the study of values. This outline itself is the fruit of several years of specialized research on a variety of value themes and problems at levels of empirical study and of phenomenological reflection.

Yet Allo's normative sequence has never been tested from beginning to end in any field setting. Therefore, one cannot know in concrete terms precisely what happens to a population which probes its value crises in the Allo mode. What is most germane to the purposes of this essay, however, is that Allo, without repu-

---

[14] The following documents describe the work of Allo's "Beirut Group": *IRFED VEC (Valeurs et Civilisations) Bulletin de la Recherche*, Nos. I, II, III, IV, and V (Mimeographed).

diating the contribution of social science, nonetheless insists that it be incorporated in a total methodology, properly attuned to the very nature of values.

What follows observation is a "post-reflection" consisting of a phenomenological/philosophical treatment which goes far beyond mere correlational analysis or statistical inference. Quite apart from the promise it holds for reducing ethnocentrism and empiricist bias, this treatment can help protect populations from having social change imposed upon them (wittingly or unwittingly) by elitist groups—native or foreign—in a manner which unduly raises the cost in human suffering and value destruction. Moreover, it places the researcher in a position of vulnerability toward the people he studies. No less importantly, it thrusts his values into the same arena of critical discourse which the values of the populace itself must enter. Above all else, Allo's method incorporates analysis into a larger framework wherein all syntheses are repeatedly tested against vital experiential perceptions.

Conclusion

Social critics in developed countries are now beginning to suspect that their societies are reaping harvests of anti-development even when they profess to sow seeds of development. Goals are usually stated in lofty and resounding moral terms, but objective and subjective improvement in the conditions and quality of life are still denied to vast numbers of men in all societies. This appears to be true even where tractors and factories abound—material gains have doubtless been registered in much of the world, but the price paid for this advance has never been tallied. At times the damage is so great that it negates apparent developmental gains: better economic performance, higher literacy, and increases in export trade. In human terms, these improvements become quite insignificant. Even in the best of circumstances, development exacts a high toll in value destruction.

If such loss is to be minimized, it is apparent that new efforts must be made to study social change in terms of its value cost to its putative beneficiaries. Somehow the limits of the permissible must be identified. This means that researchers, no less than planners, must, *before taking action,* engage in critical dialogue with the interested populace itself, taking the limits posed by that populace as their own point of departure. Such a perspective calls for drastic revisions in conventional forms of studying social change, along lines suggested by the Allo model.

A striking convergence is discernible among various experimental enterprises, all of them arising from a perception of the vital importance of the emerging consciousness of the Third World. Thus, in basic inspiration and operational criteria, Allo's research methodology parallels other innovations aimed expressly at reducing ethnocentrism and manipulation. These all place responsibility for the change effort directly in the hands of the people whom it most affects. Among these experiments one may list, in particular:

—the pedagogy of the oppressed devised by Paulo Freire,[15] who engages in cultural action for freedom whether he is teaching literacy to adults or mobilizing landless peasants around the "generative themes" of their values;
—the conduct of planning as democratic dialogue by Robert Caillot,[16] whose incorporation of masses into the planning and implementation of change is analogous both to Allo's research approach and to Freire's pedagogy;
—the practice of "open-ended housing" as a vital process through which human beings enhance their own lives. This approach, advocated by John F. C. Turner,[17] is an attempt to turn attention away from housing as a product toward its nature as a humanizing, value-laden process.

On a much wider scale, it is evident that similar goals are pursued by the popular mobilization strategies adopted in China, Cuba, and Tanzania, where the transformation of culture and the creation of the "new man" are anchored, at least in ideal terms, on self-reliance and popular participation in decisions.

In all these cases, research, education, and mobilization for change are seen as parts of a single strategy best carried out when change agents share structural vulnerability with the populace. New kinds of human relationships are thereby instituted, based on vulnerability and leading to reciprocity. For without reciprocity, neither change agents nor the people are free to transcend the value crises generated by technological expansion. Representatives of the developed world hope thereby to gain the wisdom they need to match their sciences. Con-

---

[15] See Paulo Freire, *Pedagogy of the Oppressed* (New York: Herder & Herder, 1970) and *Cultural Action for Freedom* (Cambridge, Mass.: *Harvard Educational Review* and Center for the Study of Development and Social Change, Monograph No. 1, 1970).

[16] Robert Caillot, "L'Enquête-Participation à Economie et Humanisme" *Cahiers de l'Institut Canadien D'Education des Adultes*, No. 3 (February 1967), 121-144; and "Une Connaissance Engagée," *Options Humanistes* (Paris: Les Editions Ouvrières, 1968), pp. 55-79.

[17] See John F.C. Turner and Robert Fichter, *Freedom to Build: Dweller Control of the Housing Process* (New York: Macmillan, 1972) and Turner, "Barriers and Channels for Housing Development in Modernizing Countries," in *Peasants in Cities*, ed. William Mangin (Boston: Houghton Mifflin, 1970).

The Study of Values
DENIS GOULET

versely, those from the underdeveloped world can be initiated to those sciences their present wisdoms must assimilate if they are to survive in the new conditions posed by contemporary life. Ultimately, of course, all constraints must be removed, those enslaving the "developed" as well as the "underdeveloped."

Strengthening Alternative High Schools

CENTER FOR NEW SCHOOLS

Chicago, Illinois

The authors first present a case study of student involvement in decision-making at Chicago's Metro High School, emphasizing the influence of the staff, student subgroups, and the school program upon the development of the decision-making process. They then trace patterns of development common to alternative schools, criticizing the notion of "organic growth" with which many alternative schools begin. Finally, the authors propose a constructive, supportive role for research, evaluation, and feedback to strengthen alternative schools within a framework of shared analysis and decision-making.

For two years we were involved full-time in Metro High School, an alternative school in Chicago. During this time, we taught and counseled students, negotiated with the school system, worked with teachers, helped set up community-based classes, and participated in just about every aspect of starting the school. In addition, we tried out different approaches to gathering information about the development of the school, with the aim of strengthening its operation. Since that time, we

* This article results from the Metro research program conducted by Center for New Schools, 59 East Van Buren, Suite 1800, Chicago, Illinois 60605. It represents the thought and work of many people involved in establishing Metro High School over the past three years. The section "Student Involvement in Decision-making at Metro High School" is based on the work of Stephen H. Wilson, which is presented in full in his doctoral thesis, "A Participant Observation Study of the Attempt to Institute Student Participation in Decision-Making in an Experimental High School," University of Chicago, 1972. Donald R. Moore had major responsibility for writing the article in

have worked directly with five other alternative schools, providing them with technical assistance tied closely to the information-gathering techniques we found helpful at Metro. We are now collecting information about other alternative schools throughout the country and have substantial contact with about thirty additional schools. Most of these schools have the following characteristics:

1. They are urban high schools, some inside and some outside the public school system.

2. They have either diverse student bodies in terms of race, ethnic group, and social class or student bodies composed of low-income white or Black students.

3. They have enrollments of between 20 and 600 students, small by public school standards. The typical school has a student body of 150-200 students, or a series of centers each with 150-200 students.

This article grows out of our experience at Metro and our interest in strengthening other alternative schools like it. Our analysis is probably most pertinent to such schools, but it may have implications for other types of alternative schools or for those who seek changes in established conventional schools. We first present a consideration of the forces operating in Metro High School as it attempted to involve students in decision-making. This case study, based on extensive participant observation, may be of use to other alternative schools trying to find effective ways of involving students in decision-making and will illustrate some underlying patterns of development that have been repeated in many alternative schools. Next, we offer a tentative framework for understanding alternative school development as a first step in thinking about ways to strengthen alternative schools. We conclude with an analysis of the type of research and evaluation that can help to strengthen alternative schools. This final section will discuss substantive issues that warrant study, specific research methods that have proved helpful, and ways that research and evaluation can be incorporated into a much broader process in which alternative school staff and students decide how they can best create a healthy learning community.

---

its present form with the assistance of Richard Johnson, Stephen H. Wilson, and Thomas A. Wilson.

The Metro research has been supported by three grants from the Urban Education Research Fund of the University of Illinois College of Education at Chicago Circle. Additional support from the Wieboldt Foundation of Chicago also assisted us in completing this manuscript. Copyright © Center for New Schools, Inc., 1972. All rights reserved.

Student Involvement in Decision-Making at Metro High School

Metro High School is an alternative high school without walls operating within the Chicago Public School System. A private organization, Urban Research Corporation, convinced the Chicago Board of Education to start the school in 1969 and persuaded a number of businesses, cultural organizations, and community groups to cooperate by providing learning experiences for students. The 350 Metro students were selected from volunteers in a city-wide lottery. The student body closely reflected the diversity of the total school system in terms of race, social class, ethnic group, and previous success in school. The school's twenty full-time teachers all met the certification standards of the Board of Education, although about a third were from outside the school system. The staff was young and strongly committed to Metro, willing to stay until five or six every night to work with students and to discuss problems entailed in this attempt to reconstruct just about every aspect of a school's educational and social organization.[1]

Initially, the staff shared many of the assumptions about student participation in decision-making commonly made in the alternative schools that have been started in the past few years. Along with Metro's first teachers, we felt that the lack of student involvement in shaping decisions that affected their lives was a major cause of alienation and disruption within conventional high schools. We believed that students should be prepared to take a strong role in decision-making in their later lives. We felt that a good beginning for an effective learning program with these goals would be to eliminate the restrictive rules that generally govern students' daily behavior such as dress codes and hall passes; to allow students to select their own courses within broad distributional requirements; to involve students in the evaluation and planning of individual courses; and to involve students in making and implementing policies that would affect the entire community. It is this last aspect of decision-making—*involvement at the institutional level*—that is analyzed here.

Staff (including planners and teachers) assumed that students would come forward eagerly to participate in institutional decision-making, given the opportunity. Further, we didn't want to prescribe the form that such involvement would take, but hoped that the students themselves could develop an appropriate form.

---

[1] For a more detailed description of the Metro High School program, see Moore, Wilson, and Johnson, *The Metro School: A Report on the Progress of Chicago's Experimental "School Without Walls"* (Chicago: Urban Research Corporation, 1971).

A brief summary of the major phases in the evolution of this initial idea follows.

In the first semester of operation, students generally felt that no government at all was best, but that if some form of government were necessary, the only valid form would be one based on direct representation. Consequently, a weekly all-school meeting was initiated which was supposed to function as the major decision-making body within the school. Although it was effective in a few crisis situations, the meeting proved unwieldy for making ordinary decisions. Attendance fell off by the middle of the first semester, and, in the absence of clearcut decisions by these meetings, staff meetings and staff committees became the main arena for decision-making. The staff had been meeting almost daily since the school opened, anyway, trying to cope with the many problems of the new institution, and had established committees to make decisions about evaluation and curriculum.

Several faculty members were upset with the gravitation of decision-making to the staff. After the all-school meeting failed, these staff members encouraged students to form a student government with two representatives from each counseling group (similar to a home-room). However, this organization met only once before it faded from existence.

The important influences on the development of student involvement at Metro during this crucial first semester can be organized under six major topics: students' initial approach to involvement, staff's initial approach to involvement, characteristics of the Metro program, characteristics of the school system and the city, student and staff approaches in the developing program, and variations in approach among student subgroups. Our discussion of these topics is based on data collected and analyzed in a two-year program of participant observation at Metro, using methods described later in this article. Each of the key generalizations presented in the following section (for example, that most students initially felt only governments based on direct representation were legitimate) has been developed using these methods of data collection and analysis. Quotations are used to illustrate various generalizations and are not intended to "prove" any point.

Students' Initial Approach to Involvement

We will not attempt to review other research and theory in discussing student involvement in decision-making at Metro. However, one distinction employed by Etzioni[2] is extremely useful in understanding the students' initial orientations

[2] Amitai Etzioni, "Organizational Control Structure," in *Handbook of Organizations*, ed. James G. March (Chicago: Rand McNally, 1965).

toward decision-making. Etzioni hypothesizes that organizations develop two major realms of activity: the "instrumental" realm, which is related to the official functions of the organization, and the "expressive" realm, which is related to people's personal concerns. In the school context, "instrumental" activities deal mainly with the operation of the instructional program, while "expressive" activities center around friendships, dating, athletics, and informal "rapping." In many organizations, two different structures evolve to deal with these two realms, with the expressive realm having leaders, values, and styles of action that may be at odds with the organization of the instrumental realm. In the traditional school context, adolescents often invest most of their energy in the expressive realm, and leadership in expressive activities determines prestige with other students. Administration and teachers often attempt to exert strict controls over not only the instrumental realm, but also the expressive realm, through rules about dress, social interaction, movement, eating, and smoking. To defend their autonomy in the expressive realm, students create separate expressive subcultures, and recently have directly challenged the school's right to regulate their expressive activity.

Coming from traditional schools, Metro students were very concerned to gain autonomy in the expressive realm. Metro staff strongly encouraged this direction because we considered freedom of movement, dress, expression, and association fundamental to the program's design. Thus, in the areas that students cared most about, there was no need for organized participation in decision-making. The battle had already been won. At the end of the first semester of operation, all students were asked in short structured interviews what they liked most about Metro as compared with their old school. The characteristic of the program cited most often was freedom in the expressive realm: freedom to talk to friends, get up and leave if you were restless, wear what you wanted, or eat when you wanted.

In this same series of interviews students also frequently mentioned the closer student-teacher relationship as one of the school's strengths. The staff's willingness to grant freedom in the expressive realm helped establish a degree of trust between teachers and students. Staff members were sensitive to student concerns, and by the end of the first semester many students felt comfortable in openly criticizing those aspects of the program they wanted changed. This freedom to criticize was extremely important to students; they generally preferred a decision-making role in which they could bring problems to the attention of the staff, who would then have the responsibility to develop solutions, rather than one in which they developed and implemented detailed programs themselves.

Student: The way you got to do it is to make decisions. Then if we don't like it, we'll let you know. You do something and we'll react. Students don't dig sitting in meetings and stuff and you don't have any idea what it means.

The major concerns of students with regard to school policies were: to obtain as wide a field as possible for expressive activity; to be able to complain to the staff about instrumental activities they disliked; to establish the right to opt out of instrumental activity if they wished. To a large extent the first objective was achieved. In the few areas of expressive activity where freedom was not allowed (for example, students were not allowed to smoke in the school headquarters because of a Board of Education rule), there was constant minor friction with the staff. The second objective was also largely achieved: almost all teachers were open to students' complaints and effectively communicated this willingness to listen to students, even though they did not always solve the problems posed. Many students initially felt that the third objective had also been achieved because of the staff's stated emphasis on freedom in the program.

With their major objectives largely achieved, Metro students saw little reason to become actively involved in a formal decision-making process. Staff members argued that students should carve out some formal decision-making role for themselves, since the staff might not always act in the students' best interest. This argument, however, was highly abstract, and most students were influenced much more by present reality. They saw little need to expend energy in a decision-making process when things were already going their way.

A major factor in students' reluctance to create a formal decision-making structure was their strongly negative experience with student governments in their old schools. Such governments had had limited power, had been manipulated by teachers and administrators, had made and enforced restrictive rules rather than protected student interests, and had often been composed primarily of students from higher status homes.

Student: The student council was just puppets for the teachers. They pulled the strings and the student council did what they wanted.

Student: There was one clique that got involved. No one else paid any attention.

In the face of this negative experience, staff and those students pushing student government were never successful in communicating an alternative image of what a government could be to the majority of the students.

Student: All government is is some guy going around telling you what to do. There are people here nobody is going to force them to do anything.

Student: If we have a student government, they'll start making rules and pretty soon we'll end up like the old schools.

Observer: Why don't you guys get together in some kind of student government and see what you can do about it (the lack of gym equipment).

Student: A student government couldn't do that shit.

Believing that things were going well, many students cited local and national governmental structures with which they were dissatisfied in arguing against a government at Metro. Politically active "youth culture" students cited the war policies of the national government. Many Black students cited the actions of the police at a local level. In both instances, the form of the argument was the same: "You're copying the kind of government that we already know doesn't work right."

Many students held to the notion that the individual is powerless in acting against larger forces in the society; they maintained that involvement was pointless. When they did get involved, any small setback confirmed their belief that "you can't fight the system." A role in actively planning and carrying out decisions was completely foreign to students' previous experiences; the most many hoped for was a chance to complain. Staff attempts to move students beyond the complaining mode were largely unsuccessful.

Closely related to students' distrust of governmental structures and school-wide policies was a personal ethic that is summarized in two current cliches: "do your own thing" and "hang loose." Student adherence to these ideas came through repeatedly in both our interviews and our observations. The ideal form of government for Metro, many students believed, was none at all. There would be no government, no rules; only "people dealing with people."

Student: We're going to have a beautiful anarchy. Everybody's going to do their own thing and leave everybody else alone. We decided we don't need a government.

Following from this theory, if there had to be some form of government, it could only involve direct representation. Most students felt that people could only speak for themselves, not for other people.

Student: No one can represent me. I'm the only person who knows what I'm thinking and no one else can present my views.

This aversion to representative government was related somewhat to the extreme diversity of the Metro population. However, some students felt that they couldn't even represent their best friends.

Denial of the concept of representation, linked in part to students' negative experiences with student governments in their old schools, called into question the motives of those students who wished to form a representative government. Thus, students who privately admitted that they were extremely interested in participating in a student government were reluctant to come forward for fear of being branded as power-hungry by their peers.

Teacher: Let's elect a representative. Any nominations.... No nominations? I guess we'll have to ask who's willing to be ours.

Student: (feigning great reluctance) I guess if no one wants it, I'll volunteer.

The "hang loose" ethic glorified reacting to the feeling of the moment and coping with each situation as it arose. It opposed planning, rules, and long meetings. It led students to accept whatever happened with equanimity. If no one showed up for a scheduled meeting, the likely response was, "We'll just have it another time." If the person who was supposed to buy pop for a picnic came without it, the explanation "I just couldn't get it together" satisfied many people.

The nature of the staff meetings also hindered student involvement in formal decision-making. Many staff meetings were long, marked by extended rhetorical exchanges, and conducted using procedures unfamiliar to most students. Time was spent discussing details of implementation that students felt were trivial. Attendance at a few staff meetings confirmed the belief that the best way to influence decisions was to talk informally with teachers and let them fight it out.

Student: I'm not going to spend all those hours working on that stuff. These teachers are here till six every day. They're paid to do it.

Student: I shouldn't have to worry about that. I'm getting credit for being a student, not for being a teacher.

The process of decision-making came in dead last in terms of enjoyment, well behind "messing around," "rapping," or "playing ball."

Student: No, can't (come to meeting). Me and Karen are going to mess around downtown today.

Staff's Initial Approach to Involvement

As it became clear that the all-school meeting was an inadequate arena for decision-making and as the problems of inventing an entirely new institution mounted, the staff increasingly felt that the survival of the institution depended primarily on their ability to make decisions and carry them out. Student involvement in institutional decision-making, which for many staff members had been a top priority initially, became secondary to finding solutions to pressing problems.

Given this context, many characteristics of the staff, some of which have already been touched on, lessened the likelihood of formal participation by students in institutional decision-making.

1. Staff members had a close relationship with students, were willing to listen to students' gripes about the program, and were often sensitive in reacting to and even anticipating students' needs.

2. The staff felt ultimately responsible for the success of the program; we felt that if it failed, its demise would be perceived as our responsibility, not the students'.

3. Unexpectedly, the excellence and creativity of the staff worked against student involvement. Tentative student ideas were often pale in comparison to teachers' well-developed ideas that grew out of long experience and analysis.

4. However much a staff member was consciously committed to student involvement, his or her past life experience as a teacher and earlier as a student had cast students in a submissive role. Especially when harried and overworked, staff tended to revert to old role definitions.

5. Some staff members were ambivalent about the desirability of student involvement in decision-making and unsure of its limits. They communicated this ambivalence, often in subtle ways, by their actions in the decision-making process.

6. Teachers had superior skills in the process of bureaucratic decision-making compared with students. This competence acted as a constant pressure (of which we were generally not aware) that consolidated the staff role in decision-making vis-à-vis the students.

7. Even when students were present in staff meetings, staff shaped the event. We were always there, and we knew past history of which students were unaware.

Teacher: Do you know what's going on?

Student: No, I wasn't here when you discussed it last week.

Teacher: See, that's one of our biggest problems. We'll never get anything done if it always goes on like this.

8. The staff itself encountered formidable problems in becoming an effective body for making and carrying out decisions. We had had limited experience in working in this capacity in previous teaching assignments. Personality clashes sometimes obscured issues; an initial rejection of procedural rules allowed discus-

sions to wander aimlessly; those present at meetings were often unclear as to when a decision had been reached; those absent were not always informed about decisions; responsibility was often not clearly assigned for carrying out a decision. When decisions required widespread cooperation of students and staff, staff members were hesitant to confront individuals who violated agreements. A detailed consideration of these issues is in itself a major topic of the Metro research program. However, there are direct implications for student involvement: most staff members, facing difficult problems of dealing with each other in decision-making, often could not cope sensitively with the added issue of student involvement.

This discussion might give the misleading impression that the staff knowingly throttled student involvement. The case was quite the opposite. Most staff members spent considerable time listening to student complaints and trying to deal with them, agonizing over the lack of student involvement and trying to correct it. Had the students exhibited a strong desire for involvement, staff characteristics that worked against student involvement would probably have been a minor influence. As it happened, however, they meshed with prevailing student attitudes to minimize the chances of student involvement.

Characteristics of the Metro Program

It is of course impossible to neatly separate characteristics of the program from characteristics of the students and staff mentioned above. Yet it is useful, at least for the purpose of analysis, to discuss separately several aspects of the developing Metro program that tended to work against student participation in institutional decision-making.

Metro was testing a number of new educational ideas that staff members deemed just as important as the idea of involving students in decision-making. To some extent, these ideas worked against the goal of student involvement. The school without walls concept dispersed students throughout the city and made meetings and communications difficult. The multi-racial and multi-class student body made it hard for the students to speak with one voice on any issue. The attractiveness of curriculum offerings such as film-making, improvisational theater, and internships in political organizations competed with decision-making for the student's time, as did the many opportunities for expressive activity. In addition, the school's commitment to certain curricular innovations (interdisciplinary curricula, use of the city as a learning resource) sometimes limited the field for decision-making.

Student: We told them we didn't like that core course idea and that it just wouldn't work, but it went in one ear and right out the other.

A second area of difficulty was communications within the school. Communications regarding the time and place of meetings, their agendas, and the status of various decisions were often ineffective at Metro. Sometimes meetings were advertised only through informal channels. Sometimes only staff received notification. So many signs and notices were constantly bombarding students that much information was lost and some people completely tuned out these overloaded communication channels. Many communications were of generally poor graphic quality, e.g., blurred dittoes, tiny hand-written signs, or bulletin boards with several hundred nondescript notices. This communication problem discouraged the participation of all but the most committed and undercut the legitimacy of decisions that were made without most people's knowledge.

Student: Who made that decision? I never heard about those meetings; are you sure they told people about them?

As in any institution, many of the discussions and work related to decision-making went on informally. This tendency was accentuated at Metro by the organizational confusion of the new institution and the emphasis on informality that pervaded the school. This informality had the unintended effect of excluding students from many important discussions relevant to various decisions. Even though teachers and students had close relationships, teachers tended to eat and relax together. Key meetings were often called quickly in response to a crisis or impending deadline, and informal channels of communication shaped the group that turned out.

Announcements of meetings were often not fully understood even when students heard or saw the message. Many students had a limited concept of the influence they could have in shaping decisions they were concerned about. They failed to relate their concerns to the expectation that they would get something done by attending an announced meeting. The ability to receive and comprehend communications varied widely among student subgroups, as will be discussed later.

Characteristics of the School System and the City

Metro did not develop in a vacuum. It had to deal constantly with a school bureaucracy whose reaction to the school generally ranged between indifference and open hostility. Few persons in the school bureaucracy and in the city at large shared Metro's commitment to a new vision of the capacities of adolescents. Key members of the central administrative staff of the Board of Education were consistently opposed to student involvement in decision-making, and their disparagement of Metro's efforts was often communicated to the student body. As these stories circulated, it became unclear whether the disparaging statements were made by central administrative staff or Metro staff.

Principal to Staff: I showed the plan for the administrative board to the district superintendent. She couldn't stop laughing. Teachers and students have equal votes. She showed it all around the office.

The bureaucracy often blocked or delayed the implementation of Metro decisions. Some students who participated in decision-making did not understand the enervating process of working through and around the bureaucracy and interpreted the delays as a result of the Metro staff's insincerity. Other students came to understand the process, but became discouraged about accomplishing anything in the face of this giant bureaucracy.

The nature of the "school without walls" put students in constant contact with an outside world (including elevator operators, policemen, transit collectors, store and office building guards) that gives limited rights to young people. Metro often took the student's part in these encounters, protesting to the transit authority, for example, about collectors who wouldn't accept students' fare cards. However, the school had limited success in many such instances. Again, delay and failure discouraged students from participating in decision-making.

A final and very important aspect of the larger society that affected Metro was the compulsory nature of schooling. Since students were compelled by law to stay in school until age sixteen and many were under parental pressure to finish high school, some students viewed Metro as the best of a set of limited options. Ideally, they would have preferred not to attend any school at all, so they had limited interest in shaping Metro beyond protecting their expressive activities and their right to opt out of undesirable instrumental activities.

Student: You'll let us decorate our zoo, but you won't let us out.

Student: The only reason I stay is cause my mama says I better. She didn't finish, and she wants me to. She said she'd tan my ass if I quit.

Student and Staff Approaches in the Developing Program
The main factors that influenced the history of student involvement in institutional decision-making at Metro were largely fixed, or became apparent, in the

first semester of operation. During the second and third semesters (September 1970 to June 1971), the actions of students and staff can be seen to flow largely from their initial attitudes and actions.

Near the end of the second semester of operation, a group of staff and students tried to develop a new model for a staff-student governing body. Under this plan, an "administrative board" was to become the central governing unit. The board was to be composed of representatives from "like groups" formed by both staff and students. A "like group" was any group of five people who felt they had common interests they wanted to see represented. Each like group could have representation on the board.

Over a period of several weeks, like groups were formed, procedures were established for the administrative board and a chairman was elected. The board functioned for about six weeks and then quietly expired. Three factors contributed to its demise: (1) student involvement in the administrative board was generally limited to the small group of students who had been active in past government schemes; (2) the board's initiators had hoped the board could incorporate the already functioning staff committee system and coordinate its work with the principal, but this attempt was not successful; (3) the administrative board was overly concerned about the dangers of centralization and so suffered from a lack of organization.

Once again, the staff meeting and its associated committees became the major arena for decision-making and implementation. The staff meeting/committee structure grew increasingly efficient at making decisions and carrying them out, while students continued to be unaware of its overall nature.

Student: I didn't like the way registration worked.
Teacher: You ought to get to work on the curriculum committee.
Student: What's that?
Student: What do you mean curriculum committee?

Participation was greatest in crisis situations when students discussed issues at all-school meetings and turned out in somewhat larger numbers to work within the staff decision-making apparatus. Some students did attend staff meetings regularly, and individual committees met some success in involving students in their work. However, as attempts to turn students out for meetings failed, less and less effort was invested in communicating the times and agendas of meetings to the school at large.

Strengthening Alternative High Schools
CENTER FOR NEW SCHOOLS

Student: What's that over there?
Teacher: It's a staff meeting.
Student: Can we go hear what they're talking about?
Teacher: Sure, they're open meetings. Didn't you know that?
Observer: How's the committee coming? Have any students come to meetings?
Teacher: I gave up on them. Last year, I put up signs and signs and no one showed. I guess they're not interested.

Students who did decide to come to a staff or curriculum committee meeting confronted a group of people who shared a lot of common experience, controlled the meeting, often felt harried and anxious to make progress, sometimes sent out ambiguous signals regarding student involvement, and were often reluctant to "fill people in" about what had transpired.

Teacher: You know, we've been through five evaluations now. Our committee is just beginning to feel like we know what's happening. It doesn't make much sense to start all over again. Students are welcome to come help though.

The articulate, forceful student could overcome these dynamics since most staff members still talked constantly to students about issues in the school and were anxious to know student views. However, the average student attending a staff meeting came to feel essentially like a visitor.

The solidification of the staff meeting/committee system diminished the chances for survival of the faculty-student administrative board. In the view of some staff members, those who started the ad board were perpetuating the same weaknesses that were embodied in the all-school meeting and student council approaches. Rotating chairmen, uncertain meeting times, and changing representatives reminded them of earlier decision-making vacuums into which the staff had been compelled to move. Further, some staff members who had done considerable work through the committee system on such topics as evaluation and curriculum were reluctant to throw their lot in with the ad board.

Teacher: The way I understand it the ad board is just supposed to recommend things. I don't see the use of the curriculum committee and all the work we've done if it's still got to be voted on.

As time went on, there was a shift in concern from decision-making to decision-implementation. The staff became very efficient at implementing the type of decision that required the work of a few people, such as developing a format for registration. However, they had much greater difficulty in implementing decisions that required widespread cooperation of staff and students such as a prohibition on noisy activities in the conference areas. Initially, staff members were extremely reluctant to set up clear limits for behavior and act as "policemen" in enforcing them. They had basic disagreements, which they did not start to clarify until well into the second semester of operation, concerning the limits of behavior and a staff member's responsibility in enforcing them.

The issue of enforcing limits within the school raised particular problems for students. Staff had hoped that the entire community of staff and students would enforce agreed upon "understandings." Students did feel a measure of responsibility to deal with students who were clearly out of line, particularly when their action might result in bad publicity for the school. However, students were extremely reluctant to confront their fellows, since this ran counter to the notion that everyone should be free to do his or her own thing.

Student: We'd get together in these meetings and make all kinds of resolutions. Like keeping the TV low or talking to people who were cutting. When it got down to really saying something to someone, no one could do it. It just wasn't done.

The diversity of students in the school made this problem even more severe. If students were asked how a decision should be carried out, they often responded that "everyone will take care of himself."

Student: Who's going to do it? (Put out notes on the results of a meeting).

Student: You know, whoever feels like it will do it.

Even when it was apparent that self-regulation was not working—for example, during a time when there was extensive thievery of girls' purses—students preferred to suffer the consequences rather than institute rules and procedures.

Student: I got some stuff ripped off from my locker. It's something you just live with. You don't bring stuff and leave it around. You don't want cops walking around here, do you?

Those students who did attempt to enforce community understandings were often ignored or belittled by their fellows.

Student: I'm really depressed today. Two times I tried to talk to people who were messing up. Once there were two kids chasing each other around a room. I asked them to stop, and one asked me, 'What gives you the authority to tell me to stop?' Another time there was a guy bouncing a ball against a wall, messing it up. I asked him to stop. His friend asked where was my badge. Then he said, 'Yeah, you a policeman or something?' He kept on bouncing the ball. Then he said, 'Make me stop.'

Even during the early period when important decisions were made in all-school meetings, many students were not aware of what these decisions were or did not feel bound by decisions they had not taken part in.

Student: Who decided it was going to be done that way?

Teacher: There was a student meeting yesterday afternoon.

Student: I wasn't there and I can name ten other guys who weren't. Now, you know they're not going to go along with that.

As decision-making became centered in the staff meeting/committee system, students increasingly viewed decisions as externally imposed rules.

Student: This place is getting worse. They're beginning to push us around and make rules.

It should be emphasized that most students were enthusiastic about the school and generally satisfied with its operation.[3] However, observations and interviews in the third semester revealed that a system in which students communicated informally with staff, while staff dominated the formal decision-making, had some serious short-comings. Staff were extremely overworked, and they could deal only with a portion of the complaints advanced by students. They tended to select those issues for resolution that they deemed most important in the light of their own values. Thus they more effectively served the needs of students with value orientations and backgrounds similar to theirs.

Variations in Approach among Student Subgroups

Metro probably has one of the most diverse student bodies of any high school in the United States. Students were selected randomly from a cross-section of applicants representative of student population of the city as a whole in terms of race, ethnic group, social class, measured ability, interests, and previous success in school. Since the outcomes of education in traditional schools have been closely related to the background characteristics of students, and since Metro sought to eliminate or at least lessen these disparities, variations among subgroups in every aspect of the Metro program were scrutinized closely. Originally, the focus

[3] An independent evaluation team from the University of Michigan who spent a week at the school during its third semester confirmed this observation. See Glorianne Wittes *et al., Problems and Potentials of Innovative Governance Structures in Secondary Schools* (Ann Arbor, Mich.: Educational Change Team, University of Michigan, 1972).

of the research was on racial and social class subgroups within the school. However, our observations led to some classifications for students based more directly on their attitudes, actions, and patterns of association within the Metro program. These groupings were closely related to the life styles, attitudes toward schooling and patterns of association students had developed in the traditional school:

Black School-Oriented: The Black School-Oriented students conformed to the expectations of their previous schools, in terms of both academic performance and personal behavior. They viewed school in terms of getting a good job and going to college. They tended to complete school work faithfully and had average to superior skill levels and records of past achievement. They came from lower to middle income background.[4]

Black-Consciousness/School-Oriented: These students had many characteristics in common with the Black School-Oriented group. However, they were more aware of the political dimensions of the Black consciousness movement and talked about success in school as a means for gaining skills that would further Black political development.

Black School-Alienated: The previous experiences of these students had been characterized by academic failure and conflict with the school. They identified strongly with black students from similar backgrounds. These students also identified with the esthetic elements of black consciousness in terms of dress and music. They tended to come from low-income families and often lived in large housing projects or physically decaying inner city neighborhoods.

White School-Oriented: These students had the same general characteristics as Black School-Oriented students.

White School-Alienated/Ethnic: These students had a history of past school experience similar to the Black School-Alienated students. Their family income levels fell in the low to middle range. Members of the group generally saw themselves as "greasers," and thus acted out their alienation from the school in a manner that is consistent with the values of urban ethnic white youth. They were particularly hostile to the White School-Alienated/Youth Culture students.

White School-Alienated/Youth Culture: These students, mostly from middle income backgrounds, identified with the "counter culture." They tended to be articulate and expressed radical political views. They may have recently failed in

[4] Income levels were determined on the basis of parents' occupations.

school because they were "fed up with it," but their past school records included periods of high achievement, and they were generally above grade level in basic skills.

Some students can't be clearly classified in any of these groups. Labels for the groups, to the extent of their accuracy, reflect students' orientations *when they came to Metro*. Over two-thirds of the School-Alienated students became much more involved in the program; most School-Oriented students, who were used to slavishly obeying the teacher, developed more independent styles of learning. However, even students who underwent dramatic changes in some respects continued to identify with and employ life styles characteristic of their original subgroup in the school and to interact most with students from their own subgroup.

The existence of these subgroups had a number of effects on student involvement in institutional decision-making. As mentioned earlier, diversity undercut the notion that any student could speak for a significant number of his/her fellows. Further, when a nucleus of students formed around an issue, they generally represented one subgroup in the school. For instance, the White School-Oriented group was interested in obtaining more college prep courses. Such subgroups were often criticized for or expressed doubts about not being representative of the school, but they found it difficult to interest students outside their subgroup in their issue.

White Youth Culture Student: This meeting is ridiculous. You're obviously not representative. Just look around and there aren't any Black students here.

Teacher: I liked what your activity group planned for the school, but you know what you got to do now—you got to let all kinds of students know about it or you won't get any support.

In the heterogeneous student body, informal information about decision-making (meeting times, hot issues, etc.) was generally shared within subgroups rather than between subgroups.

By the second semester of operation, each subgroup had developed a fairly comprehensive view about what Metro was like, how it "really" worked, and what styles of action were appropriate for subgroup members. Each had a definite view about student involvement in decision-making which it reinforced among its members and with which it socialized new students. The existence of this socialization process strongly influenced the chances that students from particular subgroups would become involved.

It is beyond the scope of this analysis to clarify the responses of all subgroups within the school to the attempt to involve them in institutional decision-making. A brief treatment of two groups, however, the White School-Alienated/Youth Culture group and the Black School-Alienated group, will give some understanding of variations in approach to school governance.

Almost every student who became involved in decision-making on a sustained basis came from the White School-Alienated/Youth Culture group.

Teacher: How come it's always the same kids who show up for anything. I haven't seen more than about eight different kids at these meetings.

They shared the class background and life style of the majority of the faculty. They were attuned to the same political issues as many faculty members and shared the same ideas about the need for freedom in education and for the radical alteration of conventional schooling. In a school characterized by close contacts with staff, they were likely to have the closest contacts. Since they were politically oriented, they generally agreed with the argument that students had to organize themselves to protect their interests. They had high reading skills and were the best tuned to informal and formal communication about decision-making within the school. For all of these reasons, it was they who were most likely to see their concerns acted on by the staff. Sometimes they created the impression, usually unconsciously, that their views represented the views of the entire student body. For example, most of the staff shared the feeling of the White Youth Culture students that traditional school activities and symbols, such as dances, class rings, school colors, and cheerleaders, were corny and unnecessary. This convergence of values obscured the strong interest among the School-Oriented and other School-Alienated groups in bringing some of these conventional school elements to Metro.[5]

The Black School-Alienated group and the White School-Alienated/Ethnic group were the least effective in getting what they wanted in Metro's decision-making process. The generalizations below can be applied with minor variations to both these groups, though they are based specifically on the data concerning the Black School-Alienated group. Many past experiences had decreased the likelihood that the Black School-Alienated group would participate in the evolving

---

[5] One interesting distinction between the traditional schools and Metro is the influence of the White School-Alienated/Youth-Culture students at the latter. Metro seems to have worked best with the School-Oriented students and the White School-Alienated/Youth-Culture students and to have had the most difficulty in meeting the needs of the other two School-Alienated groups.

formal decision-making process at Metro. In their previous schools, they had generally seen themselves as being at war with teachers and administrators. They had kept their expressive life "underground," rigidly separated from the instructional program. They had almost no past experience with the procedural rituals of formal decision-making. They had generally low reading skills and had largely turned off the traditional school's communication channels. The Black School-Alienated group had a wealth of past experiences that taught them to conserve their energy for activities other than trying to change things. What leverage one obtained in influencing one's destiny was largely the result of individual resourcefulness in seizing momentary opportunities, not the result of establishing a framework of institutional rules within which to operate.

Many students in this group changed markedly after they came to Metro. Over two-thirds became significantly involved in the Metro program. They appreciated the friendliness of teachers and the absence of constant harassment. They identified with the school and wanted to insure its survival.

School-Alienated Female, to two School-Alienated Males who are smoking: Hey, what are you doing, you fool? Do you want the Board to come down and shut this place down?

With most teachers, they were outwardly friendly but extremely protective of their real concerns. With a few teachers, they formed close relationships, and these teachers often advocated their views about the program in formal meetings.

School-Alienated Student: I can trust the ones I'm tight with. I can tell them anything.

Yet their approach to formal decision-making was influenced both by their past experiences and by the middle-class bias of Metro. They retained their suspicion of authority and put most of their energy into expressive activities. They attended few formal meetings, were often silent when they did attend, and often left meetings that dragged on. They were not reached by the school's communication system. (When staff members expressed concern about students who didn't respond to communications, their increased attempts at communication generally reached only those School-Oriented and Youth Culture students who were already attuned to what was happening.)

Black School-Alienated Student: Nobody ever looks at signs. They're always bullshit.

A counselor announced to the counseling group that there would be a meeting after school to try to discover why people were cutting classes. Half the counseling group members were cutting and didn't hear the announcement.

White Youth Culture students' attempt to avoid overcentralization in decision-making resulted in disorganization (changed meetings, unclear agendas, etc.) that further discouraged participation by the Black School-Alienated group.

Black and White School-Alienated students, as well as some Black and White School-Oriented students, wanted the limits of school behavior clarified and harsh actions to be carried out by the principal if students exceeded these limits. The School-Alienated students expressed this point of view even though some of their number would have been likely targets of this sort of action.

As leaders emerged within the Black School-Alienated group, attempts were made to involve them in formal decision-making. These students usually listened politely but indicated by their later actions that they preferred to pursue activities in the expressive subculture such as dating and sports rather than become involved in governance.

The students in this group liked many aspects of the school and had definite viewpoints about how it could be improved. However, they lacked the skills and the support from staff to work through the staff meeting/committee system. Therefore, they were often perceived as being uninterested in decision-making by some staff members and Youth Culture students or, alternatively, as not deserving of representation if they didn't turn out. The notion that people who really care about an issue will show up for a meeting exhibits a strong middle-class bias. School-Alienated students were more likely to express their dissatisfaction through socially disapproved forms, such as petty vandalism, rather than by signing petitions or attending meetings.

The Black School-Alienated group, along with the Black School-Oriented group, devoted considerable skill and energy to initiating several traditional expressive activities at Metro: interscholastic sports, dances, cheerleading. As suggested above, their interest in these activities ran counter to the majority of the staff and the White Youth Culture students. They worked with a few responsive Black staff members on these projects, but encountered two types of obstacles that weakened their faith in the school. First, they felt the Metro staff didn't give priority to their concerns, and, in a number of cases, this perception was accurate. Second, they were especially discouraged by the bureaucratic delays encountered in dealing with the central Board of Education staff, which confirmed their original beliefs about the futility of working with the system.

Patterns of Alternative High School Development

The previous section is limited to an intensive analysis of a specific school. However, in contradiction to an alternative school ideology that says that each school is unique and must struggle alone with its particular set of circumstances, many of the problems and patterns of development at Metro have recurred in other alternative schools.[6] The presence of these strong observable similarities raises two important questions:

1. What is the best way to identify and analyze common patterns in the successes and failures of alternative schools?
2. How can we use such information to strengthen alternative schools?

The remainder of the article addresses these two related questions within a tentative framework for considering the *current status* of alternative schools.

In discussing alternative schools, we find it helpful to distinguish among *process goals, outcome goals,* and *specific practices intended to achieve these goals.*

Process goals, or ideas about the qualities of a healthy learning environment, are valued partly because they are expected to foster certain outcomes, but they are also valued for their own sake. This viewpoint stems from the assumption, common to many alternative schools, that school should not be considered merely as preparation, but as a crucial life experience in its own right. Thus, alternative school people often describe a desirable learning community in terms of characteristics like the following:

1. A close relationship based on mutual trust and understanding exists between students and staff.
2. Community decision-making is shared through active participation by students, parents, and staff.
3. The human and physical resources of the entire city become a major resource for learning.
4. The characteristics of the traditional curriculum and educational program are completely reconsidered. Irrelevant subject matter designations, grading procedures, and age divisions are either fundamentally changed or eliminated so that learning becomes a more natural and coherent activity related to individual needs and concerns.
5. Students assume a major role in determining the nature and direction of their own learning.

---

[6] Reactions to this study of decision-making at Metro by people working in other alternative schools, along with the results of a recent conference where common problems encountered at seventeen alternative schools were analyzed, underscore these similarities. See Center for New Schools, "Decision-Making in Alternative Schools: Report from a National Conference" (mimeographed, 1972).

6. Students from diverse cultural backgrounds work together effectively and respect each other.

In addition to such process goals, alternative school initiators articulate various outcome goals—capacities they feel students should have when they leave the school. For example, many school founders hope that when students leave the school, they will:

1. Learn and act independently.
2. Effectively employ basic skills of reading, writing, math, and problem-solving.
3. Understand their own emotions and the emotions of others; possess skills and attitudes for effective interpersonal communication and cooperative action.
4. Understand social processes and pressing social issues and participate actively and effectively in the political process.
5. Feel a pride in their own cultural background, coupled with an understanding of and an ability to work productively with students from different cultural backgrounds.
6. Continue to develop strong individual interests and aptitudes.

Finally, school initiators begin with a set of specific practices they feel will be effective in achieving both types of goals. For example, many have felt that in order to promote student participation in institutional decision-making within the school (process goal) and to prepare students for active decision-making in later life (outcome goal), all important decisions about the school's operation should be made in a weekly community meeting of staff and students. To take another example, many have felt that to prepare students to live in a diverse society and to create a school community where there is respect and understanding between cultural groups, students should participate in a two-hour group counseling experience each week with a randomly selected group of fellow students.

As Metro High School's attempt to involve students in decision-making indicates, alternative schools have encountered a number of severe difficulties in efforts to realize such goals through specific, commonly employed practices. It would be premature to present any general theory about the nature of these difficulties—instead we hope to suggest ways that such analysis might proceed. However, there is one prevailing idea to which many of the problems of alternative schools can be traced—the concept of "organic growth." This key idea deserves special comment, not only because it contributes to many alternative school problems, but also because it frustrates attempts to analyze these problems. The concept of "organic" or "natural" growth suggests that once people are freed from the oppressive restrictions of the traditional school, a new learning community will evolve naturally as people deal with each other openly and honestly. There seems to be a widely shared assumption that both the individuals involved in an alternative school and the school community as a whole can rather easily shed a skin of traditional habits and attitudes, and that from underneath the old skin will emerge a beautiful new man, new woman, and new community. But the experience of Metro and other alternative schools suggests that what emerges "organically" in an alternative school is not a new person or community, but rather those deeply ingrained patterns of thought and action of the traditional society and the patterns of functioning that govern the operation of any complex organization.

The concept of organic development, when subjected to these harsh realities, has generated a similar pattern of events in one alternative school after another. The school is started in an atmosphere of high energy and good will. The general commitment to a more humane way of operating, the high level of personal dedication, and the good feeling that permeates any new enterprise carry it through a honeymoon period of six months to a year. The positive experience of the honeymoon period sustains the belief that just about any problem—student involvement in decision-making, race relations, moderately severe mental disturbance, the development of a relevant curriculum—can be solved in a free and open atmosphere with a strongly articulated commitment to interpersonal honesty.

As the honeymoon draws to a close, small bits of evidence begin to accumulate that people really haven't changed as much as was hoped. The all-school meeting fails. The school's tape recorders, which people used to be able to leave out, begin to disappear. The first inter-racial fight occurs. People begin to notice that although whites and Blacks are outwardly polite to each other, there is little communication, and friendship cliques are mostly all-white or all-Black. Severe interpersonal conflicts between strong-willed staff members surface, and their conflicts spill over into just about any issue debated in the school. Someone stuffs a roll of toilet paper into the toilet to make it overflow, and a window is broken. Some kids consistently fail to follow through on any of their commitments in classes and other learning experiences; and since these kids have had a year to get themselves together, some people wonder whether the alternative school is doing any more for them than the old school. Community or staff meetings are held, and strongly felt resolutions are passed. But in practice, both staff and students find it extremely difficult to confront individuals who don't abide by these resolutions, who persist in "doing their own thing."

One way to view this situation is as a conflict between the school's process goals, outcome goals, and specific practices. Particular schools have varied considerably in their commitment to various process and outcome goals. In some cases, there never is any strongly held or clearly stated set of goals, but rather a total faith in the process of organic development, a willingness to follow this process wherever it leads. In other cases, goals which exist clearly in the minds of the school's initiators are only vaguely discussed with the majority of students and staff.

There is also a strong difference in the salience of particular goals or types of goals, although these differences are never clearly spelled out. Thus, for example, in a given school many may be committed at a gut level to the school's process goals, but not to its outcome goals. Or one group may be willing to sacrifice just about anything to involve students in decision-making while to others the goal of using the city's resources for learning is most important.

If the organic theory of alternative school development had worked as people originally hoped, this confusion about goals would not be a serious problem. However, as direct democracy fails, as cooperative effort is frustrated, as the school's cultural bias produces group conflict, the diffuse notion of what the thing is all about produces a crisis in many alternative school communities. For example, many schools have discovered independently that direct democracy is not a feasible way to govern an alternative school and that students initially show little interest in becoming involved in any scheme of decision-making. These realizations create severe conflicts about goals and goal priorities. How much longer do we struggle along with the all-school meeting when it is clearly not working? Is testing this specific practice our highest priority or should we be looking for other ways to achieve the goal of shared student-staff decision-making? How important is concentrating our effort on shared decision-making anyway, as opposed to dealing with some of the cultural bias in our curriculum? Since students haven't come forward to participate in decision-making, do we conclude that student involvement isn't important to the growth of the school community and drop it, or do we keep after students or force them to become involved because it is absolutely necessary to prepare them to be active decision-makers in later life? When the disagreements are perceived as conflicts between various conceptions of the school's goals, then this realization provides a basis for clarification, analysis, and compromise. Often, however, such goal conflicts are perceived by the various sides as reflecting the bad faith, lack of commitment, or lust for power of the opposition.

For the "pioneers' of the current alternative school movement, the period when such conflicts surface has proved crucial. The healthiest school communities, at this point, begin to identify the shortcomings in the original alternative school ideology, to clarify and establish priorities among their goals, and to develop positive alternative practices to reach these goals. On the other hand, adhering to the philosophy of natural organic development—a belief that "whatever happens is the best possible thing that could have happened"—leads to a rather predictable continuing crisis, often characterized by harsh irreconcilable conflict between various people in the community, low morale, and exhaustion.

This phenomenon of exhaustion deserves special mention, since it is so typical of alternative schools that are a few years old and yet seems so unlikely in the era of good feeling and high commitment in which an alternative school begins. One manifestation of the phenomenon of "burning out" is the withdrawal of individual staff and students into a very narrow area of concern within the school, as contrasted to their initial desire to have a hand in everything.

Teacher: I've decided I'm just going to get the reading lab together and forget about the rest.

Student: I just want to be left alone, so I can get my credits and get out of here.

The final step in the burning out process comes when the student or staff member leaves the school. High staff turnover in alternative schools is a critical problem—in many, the staff has turned over almost entirely in three or four years.

Another disturbing aspect of the recent history of alternative schools is that while new schools are being established at an accelerating rate both inside and outside public school systems, these new schools are, by and large, repeating the mistakes that their predecessors have found so costly. Very little is being learned from the successes and problems of these earlier efforts. The unwillingness to learn from others' experiences is encouraged by the theory of organic development, which holds that each school situation is unique. Yet, as we have tried to indicate, the surprisingly similar patterns of development, including serious problems that recur at certain stages, suggest that alternative schools must begin to learn from each other's successes and failures if they are to become a viable option for a significant number of people.

We must replace the unexamined rhetoric of organic growth with a careful consideration of promising ways for reaching the ambitious goals that we originally expressed. As alternative schools begin to learn from each other, they must begin to create a *positive alternative tradition*. This tradition should provide detailed suggestions about viable approaches to reaching desired process and outcome goals. It should warn people against dissipating their limited energy in well-documented blind alleys. It can be developed without compromising the sensitivity to individual people and situations that has been a major strength of alternative schools. For example, this type of creative tradition is being developed by the open schools in England at the primary level where analysis of the goals of education, the role of the teacher, the structure of learning environments, and the nature of specific learning materials and activities has clarified key issues in a way that empowers people for future productive work rather than limiting them.[7]

The Role of Research and Evaluation

Success of such a process of clarification demands a general change in the attitudes of people in many roles within alternative schools. In currently healthy alternative schools, almost all of the staff and many of the students share a spirit of self-reflection and critical analysis. We believe that research and evaluation of a certain type can contribute to the necessary change.

There is currently great hostility to research and evaluation in most alternative high schools. As an alternative school director once said, "Anything that is worth evaluating cannot be evaluated; anything that can be evaluated is not worth evaluating." This general hostility results not only from the notion of organic development, but also from the crude and inappropriate approach to evaluation and research that has generally been employed in alternative high schools. For example, researchers have often ignored the range of process and outcome goals and specific practices designed to achieve them that are considered most important by alternative schools staff and students. They have chosen instead to judge schools on the basis of outcomes in skill achievement measured over short periods of time. We lack sufficient space to present a detailed critique of the faults

[7] The qualities of the open school movement to which we are referring are discussed, for example, in Joseph Featherstone, *Schools Where Children Learn* (New York: Liveright, 1971). One must be cautious, however, in drawing direct lessons for alternative high school development in American cities from the experience of open primary schools. A primary teacher can create a complete alternative learning environment within his/her classroom. However, an adequate alternative learning environment for adolescents requires a complex social organization involving the cooperation of many people. Thus, it is extremely difficult to develop alternative high school education one classroom at a time within traditional schools (or even by establishing a school within a traditional school) as has been done successfully in spreading open primary school ideas.

of past research and evaluation efforts and will touch on these problems only in passing. Our primary aim is to describe a positive helpful role, consistent with the nature of alternative high schools, that research and evaluation might play in strengthening their development. This analysis is presented under three headings: (1) general perspectives on alternative school evaluation and research; (2) productive methods for gathering and analyzing information; and (3) productive methods for feeding back information to participants in alternative schools. This division, which reflects the fragmentary development of these ideas, artificially separates areas that must come together in actual practice.

General Perspectives

Findings from the Metro research and feedback from other alternative schools suggest some emphases for research and evaluation that will increase their potential to strengthen alternative schools.

Studying Social Process: Productive research and evaluation activities should assist alternative schools in clarifying their process and outcome goals and the specific practices that can help them achieve those goals. To this end, any such research activities should include the intensive study of day-to-day interactions—interactions among students, between students and staff, among staff members, and between the school and the outside world. Such studies could document and clarify topics like the following:

1. Varying perceptions of school goals by staff and students.
2. Contradictions between specific practices designed to achieve conflicting goals—for example, freedom in the choice of courses that allows students who can't read to avoid all reading-related activities.
3. The success or failure of specific practices—for example, the fate of a campaign to get students to try to actively change learning experiences with which they are dissatisfied, rather than cutting out on them.
4. Adequacy of specific practices in achieving school goals—for example, the relationship between group counseling of students and the capacity of student groups to make and carry out group decisions.

The emphasis on the broad-based study of social process is consistent with several positions about educational evaluation and research.[8] First, researchers should

[8] These positions are supported not only in studies of alternative high schools, but also in studies of such diverse topics as early childhood education programs, effectiveness of specific reading methods, and the relationship between schooling and later political behavior.

base studies of changes in alternative school students on the consideration of a school's particular outcome goals rather than on the availability of standard achievement tests, self-image scales, etc. Further, studying specific outcomes of schooling in terms of student learning is of limited value unless one also studies the formal and informal processes that bring about these results. The specific practices employed by alternative schools should be judged not merely in terms of their short-term effectiveness in achieving specific learning goals, but also in terms of their contribution to creating a desirable school community.

Second, the "hidden" or "untaught" curriculum probably has a greater long-term effect on students than the formal planned learning program. To be effective, a learning program must be consistent in both its formal and its "untaught" aspects. These "untaught" aspects are reflected in the social structure of the school, the expectations people have for each other's behavior, and the daily patterns of social interaction.

Finally, analysis of human behavior in settings created by the social scientist (interviews, group-testing, experimental games and tasks) provides limited and often misleading information. A more adequate analysis must include studying the natural settings in which people carry out their daily activities.

Studying the Perceptions and Behaviors of Social Subgroups: One of the most deeply ingrained characteristics of traditional schools is their strong tendency to reinforce social inequalities between subcultures, so that first the process of schooling and then its outcomes favor the dominant white middle class.[9]

Any significant alternative to the traditional school must alter this dismal pattern. However, the experience of alternative schools to date has revealed that many of the assumptions about freedom and organic growth popular in alternative schools are, in reality, a reflection of the particular world view and economic position of the American white middle class. At its most blatant, this bias is exemplified by a white middle class teacher with a master's degree telling Black urban kids that learning to read, going to college, and getting a good-paying job aren't important. However, the cultural bias within alternative schools is generally much more complex and subtle, as the analysis of student involvement in decision-making by different subgroups at Metro indicates. In many instances, the bias seems to be based more on class than race. Even in alternative schools with

---

[9] See, for example, Jacob W. Getzels, "A Social Psychology of Education" in *Handbook of Social Psychology*, V, 2nd ed., eds. Gardner Lindsey and E. Aronson (Reading, Mass.: Addison Wesley, 1969).

no middle class students, the school's method of operation may still favor those students who exhibit middle class traits.

Thus, in investigating any issue in alternative school development—course selection procedures, communication in the school, counseling, learning experience in the city—it is important to study the perceptions and behaviors of student subgroups. In such a study, the researcher must strive to understand an event or idea as it is typically perceived by students from a particular subgroup. The researcher must also understand events within the school in the context of a student's total life experience.

Differing staff philosophies and efforts to deal with cultural bias in alternative schools (often related to the cultural diversity of the staff itself) also merit careful study.

Studying Specific Practices Needed to Carry Out Crucial Community Functions: The rhetoric of organic development suggests that many traditional institutional functions—for example, enforcing limits on acceptable behavior, monitoring success in implementing institutional decisions—need not be carried out in a true alternative community and that specific practices will evolve naturally and uniquely in each alternative school. In contrast, the experience of alternative schools indicates that the failure to perform certain key community functions will lead to continual crisis. Furthermore, this experience suggests that there are only a limited set of specific practices that can be employed to carry out necessary community functions, and that drifting along "naturally" waiting for such practices to evolve causes irreparable damage to the school community and may drain its energy beyond its capacity to recover. Robert Merton has formulated the problem in this way:

Any attempt to eliminate an existing social structure without providing adequate alternative structures for fulfilling the functions previously filled by the abolished organization is doomed to failure.... To seek social change without due recognition of the manifest and latent functions performed by the social organization undergoing change is to engage in social ritual rather than social engineering.... It is assumed that there are certain functions which are indispensable in the sense that unless they are performed the society (or group or individual) will not persist....

The range of variation in the items which can fulfill designated functions in a social structure is not unlimited.... The interdependence of the elements of a social structure limits the effective possibilities of change or functional alternatives.[10]

[10] Robert K. Merton, *Social Theory and Social Structure* (New York: Free Press, 1968).

One of the aims of research within alternative schools should be to clarify further the functions that an alternative school community must carry out to survive and flourish, and specific practices that are both effective in performing vital functions and consistent with alternative school process and outcome goals.

Aims of Alternative School Research and Evaluation: Control of human behavior is widely and uncritically accepted as the ultimate goal in the application of research and evaluation techniques to education. Some researchers envision experimental schools where precise specification of educational "treatments" leads to near-perfect control of results. Entire schools are conceived as treatments, with those aspects of human activity that cannot be controlled being considered undesirable or, at best, irrelevant noise in the system. Within this frame of reference, the evaluator is seen as a neutral and dispassionate measuring instrument, recording the extent to which perfect administration of treatments and perfect control of outcomes is achieved. In applying knowledge from advanced physical sciences, the goal of achieving complete control over the physical environment is being called into serious question. Yet, in applying the primitive knowledge of the behavioral sciences, maximum control of human behavior is still widely and uncritically accepted as the ultimate goal, with only technical and political strategy questions standing in the way.

Given the goal of strengthening alternative schools in a manner that is consistent with their educational goals, we propose a fundamentally different philosophy about the role of the evaluator or researcher, the characteristics of desirable learning environments, and the ultimate goal of evaluation or research. Rather than a "value-free" outsider, the researcher should be a committed but critical participant in a long-term effort to strengthen alternative schools. We wish to make explicit the value-commitment that is implicit in all types of evaluation and research efforts in education. As a participant in alternative school development, the researcher should see him/herself as contributing one of a number of perspectives on the school's growth within a framework of shared analysis and decision-making. His/her claims to understand reality in a special way should be modest in light of the primitive state of behavioral science research in general and the understanding of alternative schools in particular.

In addition, the researcher should see his/her role as helping to create situations that not only encourage certain types of anticipated learning or growth, but also enhance the possibilities for many types of unique and unanticipated learning and growth. The characteristics of such catalytic situations can be identified through various non-experimental research methods, but such learning situations differ fundamentally from the sterile learning environments created by those who seek only predictability and control.

The overall goal of a researcher operating within such a framework is not to control people, but rather to empower them by helping them understand what types of specific practices are most appropriate for achieving desired goals.

Productive Methods for Gathering and Analyzing Useful Information

We have found that the most fruitful method for research on alternative school development is participant observation and informal interviewing. This approach provides the most effective basis for understanding the complicated interrelationships of specific practices, process goals, and outcome goals as they are reflected in people's day-to-day behavior. It provides the best means for understanding the crucial issues of subgroup behavior and success in carrying out vital institutional functions. Finally, this approach meshes well with the style of alternative schools, where cooperation for extensive techniques, such as testing and structured interviewing, is difficult to obtain, but where people are relatively open to having a researcher hang around to observe what goes on and ask a few questions.

Those unfamiliar with participant observation methods often mistake it for superficial journalistic reporting or the recounting of random anecdotes. On the contrary, there is a rich methodological literature on participant observation that suggests methods for gathering and analyzing information.[11]

It is beyond the scope of this article to describe the specific methods we have found useful, except in the most schematic fashion. The primary "instrument"

[11] A more detailed discussion of the specific methods we have employed in participant observation and mini-interviewing (discussed later) is contained in Center for New Schools, *Participant Observation and Mini-Interviewing: Two Useful Research Methods for Strengthening Alternative Schools* (1972). Other helpful discussions of the nature and methods of participant observation (including areas of disagreement) are contained in: Roger Barker, *Ecological Psychology* (Stanford, Ca.: Stanford University Press, 1968); Severyn Bruyn, *Human Perspective in Sociology* (Engelwood Cliffs, N.J.: Prentice Hall, 1966); William Filstead, *Readings in Qualitative Methodology* (Chicago: Markham, 1970); Barney G. Glaser and Anselm L. Strauss, *Discovery of Grounded Theory* (Chicago: Aldine, 1967); George J. McCall and J. L. Simmons, *Issues in Participant Observation* (Glencoe, Ill.: Free Press, 1969); Pertti J. Pelto, *Anthropological Research: The Structure of Inquiry* (New York: Harper and Row, 1970); Louis Smith and William Geoffrey, *Complexities of an Urban Classroom* (New York: Holt, Rinehart, and Winston, 1968); W. Scott, "Field Methods in the Study of Organizations," in *Handbook of Organizations*; Arthur Vidich et al., eds., *Reflections on Community Studies* (New York: Harper and Row, 1971).

for participant observation is a person or group of persons who observe alternative school settings, ask questions, and record their perceptions as accurately as possible in a stream of written notes. Of course, this process of observing, questioning, and recording can not be carried out without some selectivity and bias. Therefore, we began the participant observation process with certain broad areas of concern, based primarily on the school's written statements about its goals and proposed specific practices. With these concerns in mind (for example, student involvement in decision-making, intergroup relations), we attempted to collect a large amount of initial data without forming specific hypotheses that would focus our attention too narrowly too fast. The basic unit of observation recorded was a behavior episode, i.e. an action by one or more persons or a social interaction related to one of the broad topics with which we were concerned.

Participant observation involves constant choice. In making choices, the observer strives to achieve both *adequate scope* and *adequate depth*. Adequate scope is necessary to take into account the variability of behavior between one situation and another within the school, on three main dimensions:

1. Variability among behavior settings. Behavior varies markedly in classrooms, informal rap groups, talks with outsiders, etc. Adequate participant observation implies the sampling of all formal and informal behavior settings frequented by school participants.

2. Variability over time. An observer who sees a school only at one or a few points in time may seriously misinterpret particular events. Consider, for example, the variation between the honeymoon period and subsequent periods in the development of alternative schools. Observation during the honeymoon gives an unrealistically positive picture of a school's potential, while observation during a later period of conflict might suggest that people had never sincerely tried to achieve the honesty and openness that they claim is their ideal.

3. Variability among subgroups. As emphasized earlier, variability among various student and staff subgroups is a crucial consideration in alternative schools. Observing only one subgroup (for example, students who enjoy talking to outsiders) will result in an inaccurate picture of the school.

Adequate depth of observation entails the ability to gain access to behavior in various settings and subgroups that is not substantially distorted by the observer's presence. To achieve this aim, the observer must attain a sufficient degree of intimacy with each subgroup without becoming so closely identified with one subgroup that access to others is cut off.

In striving to achieve adequate scope and depth, a participant observer in an alternative school faces countless choices which generally boil down to individual judgment. "Should I spend more time trying to make contact with the group of kids that is seldom at school or follow up on some interesting conversations with another group I know well?" "Should I go to the meeting of the curriculum committee, on the field trip to gather fossils, or just sit around and talk with students in the lounge?"

Through a continuing process of sensitive investigation, enough information is accumulated to develop a set of specific hypotheses about the general areas of concern. For example, through participant observation at Metro related to the topic of decision-making, it appeared that although students expressed a desire to help enforce community understandings about not making noise in quiet areas, in practice they found it impossible to control their fellows. This hypothesis tied in with a number of others regarding relationships between student subgroups and attitudes toward individual freedom and responsibility in the school.

With tentative hypotheses framed, we gathered additional observation and informal interview data related specifically to these hypotheses. Special efforts were made to seek out negative evidence that indicated whether and under what circumstances students *did* confront each other about violations of community understandings. In this hypothesis-testing stage, it was again important to insure adequate scope and depth of observation. Several repetitions of this cycle of framing hypotheses, seeking evidence, and rejecting, revising, and refining hypotheses in the light of new evidence led to the set of generalizations in the case study of decision-making which begins this article.

In addition to participant observation and informal interviewing, several other research methods have been employed in the Metro research program. This use of multiple methods allows a hypothesis to be cross-checked with several types of data, and also yields information on the usefulness of the research methods themselves. The analysis of most of the Metro research data has just started, but preliminary results indicate some further methods for studying alternative schools that seem to pay off.

Mini-interviews are short structured interviews with stratified random samples of staff, students, parents, or others involved in an alternative school. The strata selected for interviewing in different schools have been based on race, ethnic group, friendship group as revealed by sociogram analysis, sex, and length of stay in the school. We have employed mini-interviews to investigate such topics as perceptions of school goals by students and staff; staff attitudes about behavior limits in a school and the best way to handle them; student perceptions of how a school is changing over time; student, staff, and parent perceptions of a school's strengths and weaknesses; and the nature of an individual's contact with people from other racial groups in the school.[12] One useful approach to mini-interviewing is the repeated interviewing of the same set of individuals over time.

Mini-interview responses are recorded in written notes during the interview, transcribed in full immediately after the interview is completed, and analyzed by two raters who extract common themes from the responses and tabulate their frequency. These simple methods of analysis have proved accurate enough and quick enough to provide useful information at a time when an issue is still under consideration in a particular school. Mini-interviews are also a good method for cross-checking hypotheses from participant observation.

Another research method that has proved useful at Metro is the intensive analysis of a subsample of students chosen by the same sampling method used for mini-interviews. The information about this subsample in the Metro research has been collected through periodic in-depth interviews, achievement tests, participant observations, analysis of school records, mini-interviews, and questionnaires about background and attitudes. Preliminary analysis suggests the potential of using these various methods in concert for illuminating a number of important alternative school issues, since they can help the researcher tie together information about a student's classroom experience, behavior in informal settings with staff and friends, and experiences outside of school.

A final useful research tool that we are attempting to develop is a computer-based system for indexing and analyzing information collected using diverse research methods. Such a system seems essential if much of the information collected through research and evaluation is to be analyzed quickly enough to make a difference to students and staff in their planning within the school and in revising the research and evaluation program while it is in progress. At the same time, this computer-based system can handle many problems in registration, scheduling, and keeping track of credits. Although alternative school people are often

---

[12] Specific examples of the use of the mini-interview techniques are contained in the following studies by Center for New Schools: *The Metro School* (1971); "Career Study Center (St. Paul, Minnesota): A Formative Evaluation" (1971); "Present Status and Recommended Future Development of the Baltimore, Maryland Magnet Schools Program" (1972); "St. Mary Center for Learning (Chicago, Illinois): A Report to the Staff" (1972). A similar approach, employing repeated interviews of the same sample of students by student interviewers, is contained in Wendy Leebov Gollub, "A Case Study in Formative Evaluation" (unpublished doctoral dissertation, Harvard Graduate School of Education, 1971).

initially hostile to the idea of using computers, the Metro experience suggests that computer programs for dealing with these tasks can be operated in ways that are consistent with a school's philosophy and save people from hundreds of hours of drudgery each year.

As the reader can see, the development of specific research and evaluation methods to strengthen alternative schools is in a preliminary stage, and yet a substantial start has been made. The improvement of these methods for gathering useful information is another specific area in which sharing of experience between alternative schools is crucial.

Feeding Back Information

The development of methods for feeding back information to alternative school participants is even less advanced. Yet unless specific methods for such feedback are perfected, research and evaluation in alternative schools will be largely a sterile intellectual exercise. Traditional research and evaluation provides few useful suggestions for information feedback, since the usual process of reporting and publishing results is largely a system for communication and advancement within the traditional research and evaluation community itself.

A crucial issue here is the researcher's power relationship to the school. If the researcher has direct or indirect power to implement practices he or she perceives to be necessary, staff and students will begin to see the researcher as a spy and quickly close off opportunities for obtaining accurate information. In addition, such a power relationship is inconsistent with the concept of shared decision-making that operates in most alternative schools.

On the other hand, if the researcher is merely someone who makes little written and oral reports about the state of the school, experience at Metro and other schools suggests that this information will be almost totally ignored. The press of past attitudes, past experience, and current problems negates any possibility that dittoed reports are going to change deeply ingrained behavior patterns.

In contrast, we suggest that the researcher's role should allow him/her to confront the community with research findings in a forceful way without any formal power to implement his/her ideas. Concretely, this role could imply a series of development sessions for both staff and students, employing case studies built up from research findings, video-tapes, role-playing, or other techniques that can exert strong impact on school participants. For example, in one of the few successful feedback sessions growing out of the Metro research program, the research team first interviewed staff members asking them to give examples of situations where they had observed another staff member dealing with a student who was behaving in a way that was clearly unacceptable. Methods for dealing with such situations were of great concern to staff members at that time. Based on common themes in staff responses (Black students being treated unfairly, teachers who "walk by" difficult situations), case studies were prepared. Then, in staff development discussion groups, staff members reacted to the problems suggested by these case studies and tried to reach some agreement about how to respond to such situations in the future. Staff members and students are more likely to act on information presented in such development sessions if they have participated in previous stages of problem formulation, data collection, data analysis, and development session planning. Ideally, then, the researcher should mesh his particular skills and interests with the skills and interests of students and staff to increase people's ability to analyze their goals and specific practices.

Even a process of information gathering and feedback that included all of these desirable elements would still have to surmount substantial problems. First, even if the researcher assumes the role we have suggested, some people will still see him/her as a threat and cut off subsequent chances to gather information. Second, while we have suggested that information should be fed back to both staff and students, the approaches we have tried have been much less effective in reaching students than staff. Third, even though the feedback procedures we have suggested may give school participants a very clear idea of their problems and lead to a sincere commitment to change things, it is often difficult for a school community to plan and carry out effective solutions, since many problems result from deep-seated patterns of social functioning.

The alternative school movement will be strengthened not only by feedback of information within particular schools, but also by sharing of information between schools. The type of information worth sharing can be clarified by identifying common patterns in detailed studies of particular schools. Work groups with this purpose, composed of people from different schools, have already met on a limited basis.[13] Again, communicating accurate information about general problems and patterns of development in a way that will benefit alternative high schools is at least as difficult as collecting the information itself. One approach to this problem is to establish a network of advisors who would translate knowledge about common alternative high school successes and problems into direct personal consultation with particular schools, in a manner analogous to the ad-

---

[13] See footnote 6.

visory groups in British open schools.[14] Ideally, such advisors would be people who are also working directly in a particular alternative school. Like researchers and evaluators, they should strive to combine their particular knowledge and skills with those of other alternative high school staff and students, and avoid becoming a homogeneous and elitist group within the alternative school movement.

The alternative schools movement has reached a critical point in its history. The number of public and non-public "alternative" schools is increasing rapidly, and yet most of them are beginning with the same assumptions about organic growth that have proved unworkable in the past. Few are learning from the last few years' experience at schools like Metro.

If the history of previous educational fads provides any indication, the mass marketing of the alternative school idea may spell its end. Therefore, it is imperative that existing alternative schools intensify their efforts to build a viable alternative tradition in education. Perhaps a significant minority of the schools just starting can join in this analysis and avoid some of the potentially lethal mistakes of their predecessors.

---

[14] For a detailed analysis of an open school advisory group, see Educational Testing Service, *Analysis of an Approach to Urban Education* (Princeton, N.J.: Author, 1971).

Highlander Folk School: Getting Information, Going Back and Teaching It

FRANK ADAMS

Highlander Research and Education Center
New Market, Tennessee

If our judgments about educational change were based only on conventional histories, our vision of alternative futures would be constrained. We would probably come to the conclusion that a small number of school professionals and prominent social reformers have alone been responsible for initiating and maintaining worthwhile reforms.

Yet there are other histories. There is a history of modest or regional successes which do not meet the historians' standards of significance. There is a history of leaders and groups who are ahead of their time, who resist prevailing trends, but who appear in the official accounts as misinformed or malintentioned obstacles to the main direction of historical development. There is a history of "commonfolk" struggling to become, and becoming, their own leaders. There is a history of alternative educational perspectives, from utopian visions to practical classroom applications—developments too often known only to the few directly involved.

The neglect of these histories makes it difficult for those who today seek more humane alternatives to find reasonable connections with the past. Since they have little sense of the partial but significant successes of this tradition, reformers again and again see themselves in the despairing position of being the "first" to take on the collective legacy of centuries of Western education. The effort to record and

Highlander Folk School
FRANK ADAMS

understand this history does not mean that all "good guys" are now "bad guys," or that all people hidden from the official pages of history are saints, but that our links with the past and our hopes for the future are forged by the infrequently powerful and the powerless as well as by the characters of official history.

The story of the Highlander Folk School lends support to an alternative interpretation of our educational tradition. For forty years, the school has been an adult education center working with Southerners and dedicated to developing its students' capacities for both individual and group self-determination. This article, adapted from the author's unpublished manuscript, "Unearthing Seeds of Fire: The Idea of Highlander," reconstructs the history of the school from records kept on file at Highlander and from interviews with key participants. It describes the education and inspiration of Myles Horton, the school's founding and guiding spirit. It tells how Highlander pursued its aims in the labor struggles of the 30's, the civil rights movement, and, most recently, the awakening of Appalachian community. Finally, it presents some educational lessons deriving from the Highlander Folk experience.

THE EDITORS

The idea of starting a school to serve oppressed people first struck Myles Horton when he was 22, and then it held his imagination and dedication for life. In 1927, the summer before his senior year at Cumberland University, the Presbyterian Church sent Horton to Ozone, Tennessee, to organize daily vacation Bible schools. While much of the country was enjoying prosperity, Ozone's people were already deep in their own Great Depression. Greed's harvest had exploited and exhausted the natural supplies of timber and coal, and the people who did not leave the region faced extreme poverty and seemingly unending misery. Horton ran the Bible schools, but soon came to feel that memory verses, hymns, and games didn't have much real use in relation to the daily problems faced by the children or their hard-pressed parents.

Nor could Horton learn of *any* school program that was directly related to mountain people and their common problems. Horton decided to do something about the situation. He wasn't certain what to do, so he asked parents of children attending Bible classes to come to church at night to talk about their problems.

To his amazement, they came. Some would walk in the dusk several miles down the hollows knowing they would have to go home in the dark. The things they talked about were basic. How could jobs be found? How does a person test a well for typhoid? Could the stripped hillsides ever grow trees again? Horton's inability to answer most of their questions didn't bother them. Soon, however, they started asking him to find someone who did have the answers. The county agent was helpful. So was a man who knew how to test wells. Once neighbor started talking with neighbor they learned that answers to many of their questions were available right there in Ozone. By the summer's end the people were urging Horton to stay on, and not return to college. Cumberland University became at once unimportant and important. He'd learned that the people knew the answers to their own problems. He'd learned that the teacher's job is to get them talking about those problems, to raise and sharpen questions, and to trust people to come up with the answers. Yet, having been in traditional schools all his life he could not trust this way of learning. He promised to come back when he had something to offer. That fall, he was back in college.

During Horton's senior year, one of Tennessee's leading businessmen, a woolen manufacturer named John Emmett Edgerton, came to Cumberland and spoke against unions. Essentially he said the workers were wrong to think they could decide things for themselves. It was he, Edgerton, and other industrialists, who should determine what was good for the working man. Horton's understanding of the union movement was slight, but Edgerton's speech shocked him. Soon after, Horton went to Edgerton's Lebanon mill to talk with his workers, arguing that they were human beings who should exercise their inalienable rights. His appeal was spirited, but naive; it fell on uninterested, perhaps even fearful, ears. Horton himself was deeply confused and disappointed that the workers didn't rise in rebellion at hearing his arguments. He returned to the campus downcast, only to be greeted by university authorities with orders to stay away from Edgerton's mill. Undaunted, Horton went back, but again to no avail. This time, university authorities threatened him with expulsion.

After a year as student YMCA secretary for the state of Tennessee, Horton was introduced to Dr. Harry F. Ward's *Our Economic Morality* by Reverend Abram Nightingale of Cumberland County who subsequently urged him to study with Ward at Union Theological Seminary in New York. On being accepted, Horton went to New York, arriving just before the stock market crash, the creation of bread and soup lines throughout the city, and the eruption of much labor strife and violence in the South.

Academic life and Union profoundly affected Horton, too. Horton recalls that Abbott Kaplan, an urbane northerner, years later told a Highlander fund-raising gathering in New York City: "This little hillbilly fellow wandered up to New York to Union Theological Seminary to get the Word of the Lord. Instead, he

Highlander Folk School
FRANK ADAMS

ran into Reinhold Niebuhr, who was speaking with almost as much authority as the Lord, and apparently had a greater social conscience."

Niebuhr was just beginning his distinguished career when Horton arrived. He was teaching and writing with biting clarity against any over-simplification of the social gospel. In his course, as later in his books, Niebuhr attacked the uncritical idealism of social gospel advocates and liberal theologians. In response, those he criticized considered Niebuhr a pessimist, noting that even his moral man proved not to be very moral. Such pessimism notwithstanding, Niebuhr's arguments curbed the notion of inevitable progress then rampant in theological circles.

Horton was first drawn to Niebuhr because of his vigorous defense of the working people whose efforts to organize in 1929 were being thwarted across the nation. Niebuhr encouraged Horton in what then seemed just a dream: the idea of a school in the mountains for mountain people. While Niebuhr thought that his student could best accomplish this aim by becoming a minister, he did not withdraw his support in face of Horton's obstinate refusal to accept his advice. In fact, he agreed to help in whatever ways he could if Horton actually got the project underway. As Horton wrote to him as late as 1966: ". . . It was your inspiration and encouragement which provided the reservoir of strength and commitment that still keeps me going."

Horton was also much influenced during this period by the works of John Dewey, Vernon Parrington, George C. Counts, Edward C. Lindeman, and Joseph K. Hart. Lindeman and Hart had both written specifically on adult education, and were among the first to argue that adult education be recognized as a potent agent for social change. Hart, in fact, despaired over the possibility of producing significant change through traditional children's educational programs. He argued that adults must first learn how to live the new social order before trying to teach it. Lindeman's writing, which compared experiences in several countries, prompted Horton to look beyond his own Southern origins. He was only familiar with institutions in Tennessee, but now he began to look around New York and other major cities for models for what he called the Ozone Project. Horton left Union for the year 1930-31 to study at the University of Chicago with sociologist Robert Park and to learn first-hand from the experiences of Jane Addams' Hull House.

His struggle to "get some background" was given still another major push by a Danish-born Lutheran living in Chicago, the Reverend Aage Moller, who encouraged Horton to visit the "Danish folk schools." Horton previously had read about these schools. When the idea first emerged, the Danes were being attacked by Germany. Many Danes were forsaking their customs and even language in order to learn German, and German ways. This was especially true among the Danish upper classes. The first folk school started near the German border in 1844, and had as its major purpose the preservation of the Danish language. Four years later, another school started. It championed the cause of the people in their struggles against the landlords and nobility. A third, started in 1864 soon after Germany had taken southern Jutland, sought to spur the revival of Christianity among the peasants.

In the next thirteen years, some twenty-six folk schools were started; still others came later. The schools were free of government control. They were unencumbered with grades, ranking, examinations, and certifying students. Teaching was primarily limited to the "spoken word," lectures on mythology, Danish history, religion and language. Each folk school had an "emotionally charged" cause and unequivocally took sides on contemporary issues. Anyone eighteen or older could attend. Those who came supported the schools in whatever way possible—work at the school, food from their farms, money, if they had it. They stayed as long as they were able. Music and poetry were used by teachers to engage the students. The lectures were often repeated in the evening for older people who came into the lecture halls from the countryside.

By the end of the summer of 1931 Horton had earned enough money to make the passage. He went to Denmark, learned the language, and studied the trade union movement, the farmers' cooperatives, and the folk schools—many of which were disappointing because they had lost their initial vitality and sense of purpose. But by interviewing many of the older folk school directors he managed to discern four key characteristics that had initially produced the kind of school he had in mind.

First, many of the directors were unconventional educators. They were people on fire with awareness of injustice and the determination to correct it, to awaken the peasants to the misery restricting their lives. Second, the schools, each with its own purpose, sought to evoke among their students, as one director put it, "a picture of reality not as we have met it in our surroundings, but as we ourselves would have formed it if we could—a picture of reality as it *ought* to be." Toward that end, the schools made wide use of poetry and song: a revolutionary spark seemed inherent in these ways of communicating. Third, Horton found, the early schools sought to develop feelings and will more than memory and logic.

Joseph K. Hart best described the fourth characteristic which emerged from Horton's conversations with the older directors: "A folk school in America, as in Denmark, would probably center about a personality of some real teacher; a man

Highlander Folk School
FRANK ADAMS

who is capable of learning, and who can teach, not so much by his teaching, as by his capacity to learn. America's great lack, at present, is the lack of men of this sort. We have plenty of men and women who can teach what they know; we have very few who can teach their own capacity to learn."[1]

Horton now knew what he had to do: get behind the common judgments of the poor, help them to learn to act and speak for themselves, help them gain control over the decisions affecting their daily lives. He left Denmark and returned to New York City, where, with Niebuhr, he began laying plans to fulfill his dream. Niebuhr wrote the first fund-raising letter for the project, which was tentatively called the Southern Mountain School.

Horton's next tasks were to find a staff and a place. He turned to former Union Theological classmates John Thompson, a Tennessean, and James Dombrowski of Tampa, Florida. Both agreed to join Horton before the school's first year concluded, and to help him find other staff people in the meantime. Horton then headed south to the mountains of East Tennessee to find a place. Chance led him to meet Don West, a Georgia native, who also had been to Denmark and was interested in starting a folk school. West had a contract to teach a traditional school in Kentucky that year, but Horton's determination to start a folk school proved persuasive; West broke the contract. They visited Horton's early sponsor, Mr. Nightingale, who knew of a possible place. The house was on Monteagle Mountain, west and north of Chattanooga, and belonged to Dr. Lillian Johnson, the daughter of a wealthy Memphis banking and merchant family. Dr. Johnson, after studying the cooperative movement in Italy, had returned to the South, bought land in Grundy County, built the house, and started a school. Since 1930, however, she'd been talking of retirement and of giving her home to someone who would carry on her ideas of "community betterment."

When Horton and West arrived, Dr. Johnson was shocked as they laid out their plans for a school. Her approach to education and social service was structured and well-planned. The idea of an adult residential school without courses, without a planned curriculum, violated all Dr. Johnson's training and instincts, yet she relented before the insistence of the young men that education ought to be directly useful to the life of the community. She gave them a year's probationary lease, which was later extended indefinitely.

Horton and West moved into the house. They decided on a name which derived from the people, the place, and the school's purpose. In the 1930's, Highland was

[1] Joseph K. Hort, *Light From the North*. New York: H. Holt, 1927.

the popular name for Appalachia. A Highlander was an Appalachian, and, for Horton, folk was a term that had both a positive anthropological and a political meaning. The Highlander Folk School was created.

Grundy County: A Place in Need

The folk school was started in a place where the right to work and the right to live had been a constant struggle. Grundy County's problem could be traced, in part, to the Compromise of 1876 which resulted in the election of Rutherford B. Hayes as President of the United States. Until that year the South was essentially agrarian and characterized by a rigid caste system. While condoning exploitation of Blacks within the region, white Southerners generally were not exploited by industry. However, the Compromise of 1876, engineered by old Southern conservatives and determined Southern industrialists in league with Northern bankers, brought the railroads and industry into the region to take advantage of widespread unemployment and abundant cotton, coal, and timber.

Working people were routinely abused. On August 14, 1892, unemployed Grundy miners, organized by the secretive Knights of Labor, rebelled against the state's practice of leasing convicts to private coal companies. The rebellious miners marched on the huge prison stockade at Tracy City, captured it, and freed 390 convicts under contract to Tennessee Coal and Iron Company, the parent of today's giant U.S. Steel, and then burned the stockade to the ground. The convicts were put on a train and sent to Nashville, as much as a warning to the politicians as to get them out of Grundy. These hapless convicts had been used by mine operators throughout the Appalachian coal fields both as a cheap source of labor and a means to prevent or break strikes.

The next day war broke out between the armed miners and the state militia after 1,500 more convicts were set free at Inman, Oliver Springs, and Coal Creek, all mines owned by Tennessee Coal and Iron. Throughout the early months public opinion remained firmly on the miners' side. By 1893, however, the combined forces of the state and the coal companies had gradually retaken the mines, still using convict labor. But the revolt that started in Tracy City had sounded the death knell of convict leasing in Tennessee. In 1899, the legislature outlawed the practice. (Grundy men still speak with pride of the rebellion of 1892.)

The natural companion of injustice was long-term poverty. In 1938, nearly eighty per cent of Grundy's population of 2,250 families were on relief, placing it among the eleven poorest counties in the nation. Most men on the dole were miners and timber workers; on the average, their families survived on monthly

Highlander Folk School
FRANK ADAMS

benefit checks of $10.26 per person. Men with WPA jobs earned $19.20 a month, less than a nickel a meal for each member of a family of six—provided every cent went for food.

The Wilder Strike: Learning to Learn

Circumstances at Wilder, a bleak valley town over 100 miles to the north of Grundy County, provided a catalyst for Highlander. Horton heard of a mining company that had locked out striking miners at Wilder. He went to see the situation for himself.

Wilder was a company town; coal was its profitable reason for being. The town's few unpainted shacks were company owned. Miners were paid in scrip, good only at the company store, which charged higher prices than independent stores in the region. The company made weekly deductions for rent on the shacks, for a bath house, which didn't exist, and for a doctor, who was infrequently available. No matter how hard or long the men worked in the mines, they couldn't break even, much less get ahead. As their debts piled up, and food at home dwindled, their indignation and desperation mounted. Finally, they struck, without the support of a larger union.

Almost immediately, the company shut off the electricity and took the doors off the houses; it was winter and bitter cold. Horton was told that the company blew up a rotting, unused trestle as a pretext by which they could call on the governor to send in National Guard troops to protect private property. Horton figured that it cost the state more to guard the mines for three months than the company had paid in taxes for twenty years.

The Red Cross, supposedly responding to the emergency created by hunger growing daily in the community, handed out food and flour to the strikebreakers, but not to the strikers who, with their families, were literally starving. The county chairman of the Red Cross was the wife of the mine superintendent.

Having learned as much as he could about conditions in Wilder, and having arranged for students and teachers from Highlander to join in support of the strikers, Horton commenced writing letters to newspapers across the state appealing for food and clothing for the strikers. John Thompson, who had recently joined Highlander, later wrote, "I will never forget the long line of gaunt, haggard, brave people who lined up to receive the scant rations we handed out to last them a week. Each family got a pound of dried beans, a half-pound of coffee, two tins of canned milk (if they had a baby), half a pound of sugar. Those rations saved many lives, but meanwhile many babies had died of starvation."

The strike was led by Barney Graham, a tough mountain man. Nothing the company did seemed to break the strikers' morale. Constant harassment and insults from the National Guard seemed only to deepen the men's resolve to win. The company let it be known that if Horton and Thompson didn't stop bringing food into Wilder, they wouldn't get out alive. There was an attempt to bomb Highlander, the first of many subsequent attempts, and the students and teachers stood armed guard night and day for two weeks.

Horton persuaded Norman Thomas to come to Wilder and speak at a mass meeting for the strikers. His words were stirring, but the *Wilder Blues* written by Ed Davis, one of the strikers, was the hit of the day.

The strike and the violence went on. Barney Graham was shot in the back as he went to fetch a doctor for his ailing wife; once he fell in front of the company store, his head was bashed in by his killers, who then stood guard over his body, refusing to let anyone take it away until the sun set. Other union men's homes were shot into; some were dynamited. One scab was shot and killed; another wounded; six union men were arrested and jailed five months without bail.

Horton was arrested in Wilder, and charged by a National Guard officer with "coming here and getting information and going back and teaching it." It was his first arrest. He was marched off at bayonet point to the officers' quarters, where he was held eight hours before being released.

When the company couldn't break the strike, they started evicting strikers from their rented homes. This action, coupled with the loss of Graham's defiant leadership, broke the strike.

The Wilder strike had a powerful impact on the Highlander staff. The miners' words, songs, and deeds had dramatically illustrated the intense class consciousness of Southern workers. The Highlander staff, most of whom were strongly committed to ideologies, had hoped to kindle the workers' latent revolutionary spirit, but quickly realized that to accomplish this goal, the workers themselves would have to state—one way or another—their own beliefs. Highlander had to learn not to convert, but to bring forth; education not only had to serve the people, but, more importantly, had to be of the people.

Workers' Education: The Highlander Program

Horton's Christmas greetings for 1932 give a good picture of the school in those first days:

Our four regular boarding students from neighboring states have become an accepted part of the local community, and each is in charge of some phase of community activity.

Highlander Folk School
FRANK ADAMS

Four regular classes are held each week, with an average attendance of twenty to twenty-five. These classes are: psychology, cultural geography, revolutionary literature, and a course in the study of our present social and economic problems. In addition to those classes, there is a seminar on how social change is brought about. Much of our class discussion is based on information gained by investigation of actual labor situations in the Southern industrial area. Such first-hand information is obtained by both students and teachers. The people of our own surrounding communities are eagerly reading all the books we have and are asking for more. We are fortunate in having the support of our community, many of whom help cut wood and divide their meager food supply with us.

By 1936, Highlander had developed a three-phase educational program: six-week residence courses, extension work, and community activities. Workers who showed promise of becoming organizers or local leaders in the labor movement were selected as resident students, usually by vote of their locals. While the majority came from mills, mines, and farms, a few were college graduates interested in workers' education.

Workers' education in the 1930's usually meant schooling that taught workers reading skills, or some work skill. Highlander, like the Danish folk schools before it, did not disavow teaching basic knowledge, but students at Highlander were not taught to adjust to exploitation. Nor were they expected to become merely good union members. Highlander was teaching that the unions were organized to be controlled by and to serve the members, not the other way around.

The extension program operated in cooperation with the unions and the few farmers' organizations. Highlander students assisted strikers during organization drives. More systematic education work was done through study groups set up by the extension workers (students), often at the picket lines, where songs and group singing techniques were taught, both to spark determination and to build solidarity. Not only did the extension program recruit new students, it also permitted the school to keep in contact with both the labor movement and those former students who were moving up the organizational ranks. In the community activities program, old and young took part in dramatic classes, music lessons, and group dancing. The wide diversity of experiences and geographical backgrounds meant there was much information to be shared among the students participating in the residential programs.

Early Efforts at Desegregation

During the 1930's the staff at Highlander became much more aware of the plight of Blacks in the south and of the shared interests of poor Blacks and poor whites. Too often Blacks had been used as exploited scab labor to prevent the development of better general working conditions.

Even before Highlander opened, Horton had hoped to bring Black and white students together. But, in 1932, the climate was hardly favorable from the point of view of either Blacks or whites. The Scottsboro case, its defendants mostly from nearby Chattanooga, still inflamed racist sentiment. This was aggravated by the U.S. Supreme Court ruling in *Powell v. Alabama* that denial of counsel in a capital case violated the due process clause of the Fourteenth Amendment. The plaintiff, Powell, was a Black.

Thus, Horton was disappointed, but not surprised, when, in answer to his request for help in recruiting Black students, Dr. J. Herman Daves, then teaching at segregated Knoxville College, replied, "At this time we know of no student or graduate of our school who would be a good candidate or who would be desirous of enrolling with you." He added, however, "A number of us are extremely interested in your work."

Try as they might, the Highlander staff failed to attract Black students on any significant scale until 1944. But they persisted, as is evidenced by the fact that about a year after refusing to help find students, Dr. Daves himself, accompanied by his wife, came to teach a course at Highlander. Resident students, including some few from Grundy County, had been studying labor problems and wanted to talk about Blacks in the labor movement. The staff prepared the way by first talking with as many neighbors as possible, and by posting in their irregular community newsletter: "A few students, who have families to support and live in towns where Negroes are unorganized, wanted first-hand information as to how Negro workers could be organized. Following a discussion, several people from the community said that the students should get the Negroes' side."

Dr. Daves and his wife, in 1933, became the first Black people to stay overnight and eat at Highlander. In doing so they violated the State of Tennessee's Jim Crow school law prohibiting Blacks and whites eating together or staying overnight under the same roof. It was a law to be repeatedly flaunted at Highlander.

Throughout the 30's, Highlander worked to open the labor movement to all working people, regardless of race or sex, and, to this end, they were able to drive an occasional wedge in a closed society's door. The union education program comprised the major part of Highlander's educational effort at the time, and they continually stressed the practical daily damage of discrimination. If the bosses could pit whites against Blacks to keep wages low, then whites had to join Blacks

Highlander Folk School
FRANK ADAMS

for both their sakes. Eventually these discussions were more and more led by Black labor leaders in the South or college professors.

In 1940, Highlander informed all the unions that it served in the South that the school would no longer hold workers' education programs for unions which discriminated against Blacks. This first paid off four years later when Paul Christopher, regional CIO director and a member of Highlander's board, organized a workshop for the United Auto Workers. It was attended by forty union members, Black and white, from every corner of the South. The workers attended classroom sessions on collective bargaining, the economics of the auto and aircraft industry, and the UAW's postwar plans; while there, they also organized a cooperative food store. After this, Highlander began urging other unions to join the pioneering UAW. Support was soon developed from the Tennessee Industrial Union Council and the Southern Farmers' Union. Others followed.

Highlander found that the common problems which brought union people to Highlander in the first place, plus the informal setting away from home, provided sufficient ground upon which newly-integrated groups could work out their own ways of interacting and relating. One crucially important way Highlander nourished the working out of new interpersonal relationships was through music, usually organized by Horton's wife, Zilphia Horton.

As in Ozone years earlier, Horton found that song and dance sparked people with determination and self-assurance in ways that no other communication could. Moreover, his wife was uniquely gifted in bringing people together through music, and in helping people to express themselves by writing their own music. Perhaps the most striking example is the song brought by two union members from South Carolina that she, with folk singers Pete Seeger and Frank Hamilton, modified. The song was "We Shall Overcome."

Highlanders' Frustration: Fear at the Top

Toward the end of World War II the unions, pledged to no-strike policies for the duration of the conflict, began plans to rapidly expand membership. Those decisions had a local and regional impact. The unions were once again on the move. Highlander reflected this: Horton temporarily took on the job of organizing and developing educational programs for small farmers in Tennessee for the National Farmer's Union; the Tennessee Citizens Political Action Committee was formed at the school in 1944 when sixty delegates, representing twenty-four national unions, gathered; three labor conferences attracted over 280 Southern union delegates to Highlander that year; over 100 students, all sent by their locals, came for month-long resident sessions on labor problems.

These residential students helped run Highlander through a council of workers which was reconstituted each term. In this way, they gained practical knowledge of parliamentary procedures, public speaking, community relations, the making of posters and leaflets, and the writing of news releases and shop papers. In short, how to build a strong local.

Many of the goals shared by Highlander and the unions were attained: union membership increased throughout the South and across the nation; the procedures of the War Labor Board and the "maintenance of membership" clauses added stability to that membership; wages rose, sometimes jumped, and integration of the unions was on the rise. But where, asked Highlander staffers, was the political consciousness of the workers?

Highlanders' early hope that the union movement, especially the CIO, would become a powerful force for social and economic change had dimmed with experience. Any struggle on behalf of the working class had been submerged beneath a bureaucratic struggle for power. By 1949, an organization which had thrived on militancy was fearful of militancy, afraid the bottom might upset the top.

Highlander had joined the union movement when, as John L. Lewis wrote in an introduction to one of Zilphia's union songbooks, "it was a singing army." To many on Highlander's staff and board, though certainly not all, labor's antidemocratic impulse reached its zenith in 1949 when the CIO convened in Cleveland, Ohio, its main order of business to expel ". . . members of the Communist Party, any fascist organization or other totalitarian movement . . . or any person or organization who consistently aided other organizations to accomplish their own purposes rather than the objectives and policies set forth in the constitution of the CIO. . . ." The convention expelled two unions, the United Electrical, Radio and Machine Workers, and the Farm Equipment Workers, for "communism." Also, it withdrew from the allegedly communist-dominated World Federation of Trade Unions.

Believing that the bureaucrats who controlled the unions were using red-baiting simply to preserve the status quo, Horton predicted that ten years would pass before a single top CIO leader left office. He was wrong. It was eleven.

Highlander itself felt the weight of the approaching red purge weeks before the Cleveland convention. The school was notified in July that the union would not

Highlander Folk School
FRANK ADAMS

hold its usual workers' term at Highlander that year because, "rightly or wrongly, some leaders were of the opinion that at Highlander there exists some left-wing 'communist' influence."

Despite CIO displeasure, Highlander continued its support of the Mine, Mill and Smelter Workers, then one of the last militant unions in the South. The CIO sent out a directive telling locals to stop using Highlander, but Highlander's association with the unions did not end quite yet. There were few enforcement powers in the CIO's constitution, thus their threat of non-support was difficult to carry out. In fact, two years after the bitter exchange between the national union hierarchy and Highlander, Horton was asked by the United Packinghouse Workers, an affiliated union, to become their director of education.

Civil Rights: A New Highlander Priority

Horton's work with the UPW was Highlander's final fling with the union movement, however. Developments in the South were as much a reason for the change as disappointment at Highlander with the union movement. By 1950, Grundy County had joined much of the rest of the South in emerging from the worst of its economic ills. Not every Southern worker had a full stomach or a decent paying job, not all their children attended decent schools, but more did than didn't. Since there was little indication that the unions would go beyond these limited attainments, it was time for a shift in Highlander's priorities—away from the union movement and toward interracial progress.

In 1953, Dr. George Mitchell, who headed the Southern Regional Council in Atlanta and who was chairman of Highlander's board, told the school's annual policy-making meeting: "The next great problem is not the problem of conquering poverty, but conquering meanness, prejudice, and tradition." Highlander could become "a place in which this is studied, a place where one could learn the art and practice and methods of brotherhood." Dr. Mitchell specifically urged them to explore the problems which might occur should the U. S. Supreme Court, before whom the famous *Brown vs. Board of Education* was then pending, rule to end segregation in the public schools and/or enforce the separate but equal facilities decision. Consequently, Highlander sponsored two summer workshops for "men and women in positions to provide community leadership for an orderly transition from a segregated to an unsegregated public school system in the South."

To Make the Tongue Work

Two quite separate events in the early 1950's accidentally resulted in what Horton considers Highlander's single most important contribution to the civil rights movement and, broadly, to the field of liberal adult education.

First, in 1953, Highlander received a three-year grant from the Schwartzhaupt Foundation "to increase participation in local and national affairs, in stimulating interest in community problems, and in changing attitudes which limit democracy." In essence, the grant allowed freedom to experiment in adult education.

After two experimental efforts failed, other opportunities arose. In 1955, one of Highlander's students, Mrs. Septima Poinsette Clark, was "let go" by the Charleston School Board. Mrs. Clark had been actively encouraging Blacks to vote. Her second unpardonable transgression was accepting social invitations to the home of Judge and Mrs. Waring, patricians made pariahs by the judge's decision that South Carolina Blacks had a right to vote. After she was fired Mrs. Clark came to Highlander as director of education. It was in this capacity that she introduced the school to Esau Jenkins of Johns Island, South Carolina.

Set off from Charleston by the brackish Stono and Kaiwah rivers, the island was segregated by race in the 1950's, as it had been for some time. It was further divided by tongue—the whites spoke Charlestonese, a Southern dialect peculiar even to other native-born Southerners, while the Blacks spoke mostly Gullah, a dialect that bore traces of an African Gold Coast language spoken before the days of slavery. Mrs. Clark first went to Johns Island to teach in the 30's. The island's 3,000 Blacks fished and gardened when they could, but most of the time they worked hard in bountiful fields that weren't theirs. Sickness, illiteracy, disease, and superstition were common. Education was scarce, at least for Blacks. Mrs. Clark was eighteen when she was assigned to a two-room schoolhouse which was badly in need of repair, if not space. Over 130 students, ranging in age from six to sixteen, filled the schoolhouse wall to wall. For her duties, Mrs. Clark was paid $35 a month. Her white counterpart taught three students in a well-furnished, well-kept schoolhouse and was paid $85 a month.

On Mrs. Clark's second visit to Highlander in 1954, she brought along several people from the Charleston area, among them Esau Jenkins. For Jenkins, the immediate problem was literacy education. He told them that "so many people here (on Johns Island) can't read and write and I know this condition because I would have been almost in the same condition if I didn't go back to school."

Highlander Folk School
FRANK ADAMS

He asked Horton if Highlander would set up night schools for adults "to help them become better citizens."

Over the years, Jenkins himself had tried to do the same, but one man wasn't a school. He operated a bus from Johns Island to Charleston carrying people to their jobs and decided to get a group in the bus in the mornings and teach them how to read the part of the state constitution they would have to read to become registered voters. In this way, in twos and threes, Jenkins had added a handful of Blacks to the voting rolls. But this just scratched the surface.

With the Schwarzhaupt Foundation's money, Horton spent six months visiting Johns Island, listening to the farmers, fishermen, maids, and field hands, in an effort to learn the ways of island life.

Gradually, he learned that the islanders were ill at ease in the state's adult literacy program for some very simple, but not so obvious reasons. For one thing, the adults didn't fit into the classroom chairs. They'd been designed for children. Not only were the adults who attended uncomfortable, but they were called "Daddy Long-legs," and there was just enough deprecation in the nickname to cause embarrassment, just enough embarrassment to cause a prideful man or woman to quit. In just the same way, they were being taught as children: step-by-step; a-b-c-d; "the ball is red"; "New York is a big city." They were being asked to delay reading sentences useful to them until they could read sentences of dubious value to children. It seemed very far from the Constitution. The few who had enrolled just stopped going to classes.

Horton concluded that if Highlander were to respond to the request to "start a night school for adults," then that school would have to be outside the traditional school room and would have to be in a setting, or settings, more familiar to adults. Moreover, the work of learning to read had to be adult work. At the end of three months and thirty-six classes in all, the first fourteen students took the voting test. Eight of them were registered. And before the first Citizenship School ended, its size had more than doubled from fourteen to thirty-seven, just the opposite of the "regular" reading school.

Jenkins later told Guy Carawan of Highlander what happened next:

And then the people on Wadmalaw and Edisto Islands found out later the reason for Johns Island was so successful in registering Negroes. They ask me if it's possible to help them to get an adult school. So the next year when I went to Highlander, when it comes time for immediate problem again, I brought in Wadmalaw and Edisto, and they again say they will help if I can find a place and the teachers. I found the place, and today Wadmalaw registered more Negroes than ever registered in the history of Wadmalaw.

The same thing is happening on Edisto and all over the county. In 1954, in the county, there were 'round five or six thousand Negroes registered. In 1964, almost fourteen thousand. So everybody is jubilant for the Highlander Folk School, who have helped them see the light.

In 1963, seven years after the first Citizenship School began, figures totaled by the Southern Christian Leadership Conference, which by then was running the program, indicated that since they had taken the program over in 1960, nearly 26,000 Blacks in twelve Southern states had learned to read enough to register. SCLC also reported that volunteer teachers were at that time running over 400 Citizenship Schools across the South for over 6,500 adults. In all, Mrs. Clark estimates that nearly 100,000 learned to read and write as a result of the program.

Highlander's role on Johns Island, South Carolina, was that of a catalyst: providing the educational experience, what money was necessary, and recruiting and training teachers. Horton never entered a Citizenship School classroom as a teacher, and, as the idea spread, he discouraged other well-meaning whites from doing so, too. He felt the presence of any white stranger in the classroom altered, even stopped, the naturalness of learning. Citizenship Schools were run by Blacks from the start.

Success Invites Repression: Tennessee vs. Highlander Folk

The inevitable happened. Highlander drew fire from Southern white racists. On the celebration of its twenty-fifth anniversary, Labor Day weekend of 1957, about 180 Southerners gathered to renew their friendship, talk about the South, and share their thinking about how Highlander could strengthen its role. Among those that visited were Aubrey Williams and the Reverend Martin Luther King, Jr. Also amongst the crowd was Abner Berry, a writer from the *Daily Worker,* and Ed Friend, an undercover agent for Governor Griffin of Georgia. Berry's unwanted and apparently contrived appearance in many of Friend's photographs—including one of Horton, Aubrey Williams, Dr. King, and Rosa Parks—gave much grist to the anti-Highlander propaganda mill. Undercover agent Friend's report and this photograph, 250,000 copies in all, were subsequently sent throughout the South and the nation by Governor Griffin's Georgia Commission on Education, a tax-funded body he'd set up to root out any deviation from segregation. In an "editorial comment" accompanying the broadside, the governor stated, "It has been our purpose, as rapidly as possible, to identify the leaders and participants of this Communist training school and disseminate this information to the general pub-

Highlander Folk School
FRANK ADAMS

lic. It behooves each of us to learn more of Communist infiltration and the direction of Communist movements. Only through information and knowledge can we combat this alien menace to Constitutional government."

By the first week in October, the slick broadside, which included the photo of Horton, Dr. King, Rosa Parks, Williams, and Berry had been distributed throughout the nation. Shortly, billboards using the photo started appearing across the South, claiming in huge lettering that "King attended a Communist Training Center." Postcards using it still circulate through the mails. Years later, when Horton rejoined the Council of Southern Mountains, a board member, disgusted about Horton's re-election, sent in his resignation on one of them.

Though Governor Griffin subsequently retired, Ed Friend and his undercover work came back to haunt Highlander. He was called to testify against Highlander several years later, and brought along a twelve-minute film he'd made at the twenty-fifth anniversary.

To a degree, Governor Griffin's calumny backfired. The anniversary proved to be Highlander's highwater mark for publicity. *Time* magazine noted the event. The *Christian Century* described Griffin's attack as work "shadowed through . . . distorting prisms . . . sad and sordid enough if it stayed south near whatever paranoid minds nurture such deceit." And on December 22, the *New York Times* carried a statement released by Highlander and signed by Mrs. Eleanor Roosevelt, Dr. Reinhold Niebuhr, Monsignor John O'Grady, then head of the National Conference of Catholic Charities, and Lloyd K. Garrison, former dean of the University of Wisconsin Law School:

The attempt of the Georgia governor's commission to draw from the serious and fruitful deliberations of this gathering sustenance for the efforts of Southern racists to equate desegregation with communism evokes our strong condemnation. This kind of irresponsible demagoguery is obviously designed to intensify the difficulties confronting decent Southerners who might otherwise give leadership in the adjustment necessary for the desegregation which is inevitable. We deem it morally indefensible for any men or group to inflict upon such institutions as Highlander and upon such individuals as the respected leaders, both white and Negro, who attended the Labor Day Seminar, the damage to reputation and position which may result from the wide distribution of this slanderous material.

Highlander's hide proved tougher than the governor expected. And so the Commission on Education turned to other "problem" areas.

Highlander played a significant role in the civil rights protests of the next few years. However, to be consistent with its past and realistic about its present, Highlander had to work behind the Black movement. With perhaps as much gut instinct as analytical insight, Horton realized Highlander could help lay the groundwork for the struggle, but they couldn't much take part in it. They were white and the struggle was Black. Even more important, the leadership was now Black. The people were leading themselves.

Highlander had to figure out ways to respond to those requests for help which moved the social forces in collective directions, while ignoring those which would foster continued individualism.

Specifically to aid the Black movement, Highlander turned the Citizenship School program over to SCLC. As educators, Highlander's staff felt that to continue administering an already established program would hamper their ability to experiment with new approaches. And they believed that a strong educational program linked to a forceful organization would help to build the organization's leadership potential.

There was still another major reason for giving the program over to SCLC in 1960. The year before Highlander had been seriously threatened with revocation of its charter by an investigation conducted by a committee established by the Tennessee state legislature. At the time of the decision, Highlander had been charged with being a place where people engaged in "immoral, lewd and unchaste practices," the scene of "loud, boisterous gatherings," engaging in the sale and consumption of "intoxicating liquor," breaking a 1901 state law forbidding Blacks and whites from going to school together, and, finally, that Horton "operated the school for personal gain." A trial was scheduled.

Shortly after turning the Citizenship Schools over to SCLC, Horton was free to fulfill the roles he thought proper: responding to requests for educational work only when Blacks requested it and fighting for Highlander's survival. Not long after, the State of Tennessee seized the school's property and revoked its charter. The idea and institution were reorganized and rechartered under the present name, Highlander Research and Education Center, Inc., and relocated in Knoxville.

The reorganized institution continued the policy of training community people to become leaders with a major emphasis on helping those interested in the voter registration movement, especially supporting the activities of SNCC in Mississippi. Literally dozens of workshops were run at the Center and in various parts of the South during the next few violent and crucial years of the civil rights drive.

A Glimpse of the Future

By 1964, Horton was trying to get Highlander out of the civil rights movement and back into Appalachia, and to encourage the civil rights movement to become

Highlander Folk School
FRANK ADAMS

a means by which all suppressed people in America could challenge their oppressors. It was slow work.

Horton foresaw the day when Blacks would tell whites to get out of the movement, to let them run their own show. Yet Horton continued to push the civil rights movement's leadership to go beyond their own concerns and link up with all of the nation's oppressed. The last conversation he had with Dr. King in March, 1968, only days before King was slain, is recorded in a letter he wrote the Reverend Andrew Young upon returning to Knoxville:

I believe we caught a glimpse of the future at the March 14 meeting called by SCLC. We had there in Atlanta authentic spokesmen for poor Mexican-Americans, American Indians, blacks, and whites, the making of a bottom-up coalition . . . .

Highlander continued its involvement by holding annually a five-day workshop where Mexican-Americans, Blacks, Puerto Ricans, American Indians, and whites from Appalachia could get together to talk about common problems. But since 1964, Highlander has been involved primarily in Appalachia, experimenting and evaluating ways to put education to use for perhaps another social movement.

Starting Where the People Are: The Development of Highlander's Educational Style

While Highlander has attempted to mesh the social and physical setting to make the school a way of life, it was no Utopia in the early years. The staff was young, constantly changing and usually in desperate want of money: thus the pressures and tensions were severe. Petty annoyances often became major sources of friction. Outspoken staff assertions of ideology, coupled with an inability to let the students speak their own minds, sometimes led to difficulties. On the whole, however, the staff tried to live in a way which would demonstrate for the students the sort of new social order they envisioned: one built on brotherhood, democracy, and cooperation. As Horton wrote Jim Dombrowski, before he arrived at Highlander in 1933:

If I understood our purpose correctly, we will all be working at the same job but will be using different approaches. Our task is to make class-conscious workers who envision their roles in society, and to furnish motivation as well as technicians for the achievement of this goal.

In other words, we must try to give the students an understanding of the world in which we live (a class-divided society) and an idea of the kind of world we would like to have. We have found that a very effective way to help students to understand the present social order is to throw them into conflict situations where the real nature of our society is projected in all its ugliness. To be effective, such exposure must be preceded, accompanied by, and followed by efforts to help the observer appreciate and digest what he has seen. This keeps education from getting unrealistic. While this process is going on, students need to be given an inkling of the new society. Perhaps this can be done best by having a type of life that approaches as nearly as possible the desired state. This is where our communal living at the school comes into the picture as an important educational factor. The tie-in with the conflict situations and participation in community life keeps our school from being a detached colony or utopian venture. But our efforts to live out our ideals makes possible the development of a bit of proletarian culture as an essential part of our program of workers' education.

The Highlander staff had begun as rank romantics and idealists. Theirs was a vision of the new workers' world, one where production was for use and need, not profit; where government was of and for the people; where children were well-fed. But the dreams of the Highlander staff did not make room for the people themselves. The people living around Highlander and attending from various parts of the South didn't care about education; they didn't want to build a new society. They wanted food and jobs. To Highlander's young staff, food was just an excuse for communal participation and jobs seemed almost incidental to union-building and cooperative organization. They were at first disillusioned when they proposed a cooperative to grow potatoes, ordered seed potatoes for the planned-for garden, and found that the people ate the seed as soon as it arrived. Slowly, from this and a host of similar experiences—which each staff member had to assimilate himself or herself—they came to realize that if the school was going to teach poor people, the staff would have to start the learning process at that point in their lives where the students were confronted with an immediate problem; moreover, the problem had to be one which they, the individuals or community, not the school, perceived.

In this respect, as far as institutions can, Highlander had to open itself to learning. All the staff had to learn a new tempo of interpersonal relationships, much different than their own middle-class experience. For one thing, the people were reticent and quiet. Only as they understood the people and their way of life could the staff find enough security within themselves to move away from traditional academic methods. Once they stopped trying to teach the way they'd been taught, mutual learning could begin.

Having come to question their own traditions, there was a temptation for the Highlander staff to go all the way, to reject all tradition, even their individuality.

Highlander Folk School
FRANK ADAMS

"To share their poverty, live in their cabins, assuming that to pick at bed ticks and lice while going hungry is to somehow 'be as one' with the poor is false logic," Horton argued. You could walk a mile in another man's shoes, but you couldn't wear them for life. Horton and others rejected this approach.

There were other "practical" matters to learn before Highlander's effectiveness was fully felt. At one point, soon after the Wilder strike, they were asked to organize an employment agency. At first blush, the notion had appeal. The idea came from the local community, and, if it worked, would be of use to them. However, the staff refused. They said that their goal was to help workers unite with other workers for common strength, not to help a few individuals rise above the rest. An employment agency, as such, would have added little to the community's collective strength, no matter how many individuals advanced because of it. By refusing, they taught something about mutual aid among people, and tried to attack the dilemmas of individualism.

This was one instance among many of the tension at Highlander between individualism and collective action. While the individualistic impulse could come from the students, it was just as likely to arise in the staff. Horton, despite his intellectual commitment to socialism and collective solutions, held to an abiding belief in individualism. Passages he copied as a student from John Stuart Mills' essay *On Liberty* remain in his files today.

He who lets the world, or his own portion of it, *choose his* plan of life, has no need of any other faculty than the *ape-like one of imitation.* He who chooses his plan for himself, employs all his faculties. He must use observation to see, reasoning and judgment to foresee, activity to gather materials for decisions, discrimination to decide, and *when he has decided, firmness and self-control to hold his deliberate decision.*

If a person possess any tolerable amount of common sense and experience, *his own mode of laying out his existence* is the best, not because it is the best in itself, but because it is *his own mode.* (Italics are Horton's.)

Of course, part of the impact of this strain of Horton's thought was positive, for he insisted that students at Highlander establish *their own modes* of existence and share them with the collectivity. This insistence often found fruit first through collective approaches to education. "Peer teaching" was one such method. A worker coming into his own could also help his fellow workers. Horton learned this from Dolf Vaughn, a "blacklisted" miner, who related information to students which they would use, almost immediately, in spite of previous efforts by other staff members to share the same information. Vaughn was a bridge between staff and workers. Formally educated staff members, it turned out, were never as effective in teaching as the people themselves, once they saw themselves as teachers.

At times, when the workers were facing failure and feeling inadequate to make their own decisions, there were poignant displays of the conflict between professionals advising people directly and encouraging them to decide their own fates. The problem was put most clearly to Horton during an extended and bitter strike during 1937 at a cotton mill in North Lumberton, North Carolina. After the strike had begun, Horton moved to North Lumberton to support it.

In spite of the fact that Horton and the local leadership carefully set up committees charged with the responsibility for making decisions about welfare, recreation, or the strike itself, the people weren't experienced in the business of decision-making. Horton kept telling them their union would only be as strong as their decisions made it. He rarely took part in committee work. He would make suggestions, point out alternatives, or furnish additional information. He never pushed a committee to a decision. Nonetheless, his suggestions, alternatives, and information carried added weight, especially during the strike's early days.

He was making some progress on this problem during his last weeks in Lumberton. The strike committee was meeting at a moment when it appeared as if the company was going to win. The committee had been unable to reach a conclusion on what steps to take next. There was collective anger when Horton refused to offer a suggestion. "My answer might be better than yours," he said. "Or it might be worse. But it would just be one man's answer. If I make this decision, what will you do when I'm not here and you are faced with tough decisions?"

One man started crying. Another, in desperation, pulled a pistol on Horton.

"You son of a bitch," he yelled, "you are going to tell us what to do." Horton was too startled to respond instantly. Other committee members got the weapon from their fellow member and sat him down. Eventually, as tempers cooled, the committee reached a decision on their own, learning, in the process, that they could decide on issues, and had to. In the end the tactics that were developed were successful and the union members won the right to an election and a contract.

Conclusion: The Highlander Idea

Through Highlander's programs, many people have been encouraged to find beauty and pride in their own ways, to speak their own language without humiliation, and to learn of their own power to accomplish self-defined goals through social movements built from the bottom up.

People learn of unity by acting in unity. They learn of democracy by acting democratically. And each time they do these things as a result of experiences at

Highlander Folk School
FRANK ADAMS

Highlander they both renew their capacity to act in these ways again and demonstrate the process of education in action. Talk about this process distorts, and is one step removed from the essential element—the people themselves doing. Writing words about the process is two steps removed. Education at Highlander is a synthesis of person, group, time, place, purpose, and problem. Words and sentences, spoken or written, tend to order this synthesis and give it logic by making it a sequence, when, in fact, it cannot be and is not sequential or logical. There are, of course, methods within this context, and it is these methods which Highlander has been refining with each new experience.

Baffled by education without assignment or examination, without the learned doing the talking and the unlearned the listening, some critics have described Highlander's residential workshops as anti-intellectual gatherings where the exchange of anecdote passes for education. They overlook the fact that Highlander is dedicated to helping develop the fulfillment of democracy, not to the preservation of academic discipline. They ignore that what is learned at Highlander is usually tested in real life, under the eye of unrelenting opponents, not in the classroom under the eye of a tutor.

Highlander changed its focus from workers' education and union organizing in the thirties to involvement in civil rights in the fifties and sixties and to community organizing in Appalachia in the seventies. In each stage of its history Highlander has had to combat what can only be termed repression—calumny, accusations, and arbitrary use of the legal system by local and state authorities. This has included harassment by local American Legionnaires in 1935, threats from the "Grundy County Crusaders" in 1940 and investigation by the House Un-American Activities Committee, and prosecution by the state of Tennessee in 1959 which led to the revocation of Highlander's charter and the confiscation of its property.

Highlander has survived, despite arson, arrests, and eviction. And it adjusted, in a changing political climate, to new sets of students and problems. It would be hard to lift out of the historical account of the Wilder strike and Highlander's early days, or out of its later history, a precise set of principles we could call the "Highlander idea." Yet we can make some reasonable judgments. At the least, Highlander can be described as an adult residential center in the South for the development of community leaders among school, church, civic, labor and farm groups, and for liberal education. And we can say with assurance that Highlander is committed to democracy, brotherhood, mutuality, and united social action. But it is deliberately vague about those governing concepts, letting the people it serves and the times they live in define precisely what they mean. These ideals change as people change and Highlander changes with them.

Community Power and Student Rights:
An Interview with Arthur E. Thomas

Law has traditionally influenced education through the precedent-setting power of key judicial decisions. The Tinker[1] and Serrano[2] judgments, to name only two, have generated new concepts of what student rights and educational equality might mean. Within this framework, a citizen petitions the courts with the expectation that the decision will affect individuals across the country with similar grievances. Judicial decisions can thus be used as instruments to initiate large-scale changes in policy.

During the past year, the Center for the Study of Student Citizenship, Rights, and Responsibilities in Dayton, Ohio has been exploring additional strategies for using the law to promote significant social and educational changes. Rather than relying on the legal profession to secure rights for others, the Center relies on the ability of students, parents, and citizens in the community to understand and use the law for themselves. This gives the phrase "taking the law into their own hands" a new meaning: by learning to handle the law, people can gain a sense of efficacy in dealing with their present situation and can envision new possibilities for their individual and collective futures. In this way, the law is transformed from an alien tool that controls and represses to a resource for self-construction and for confrontation with the social and political world.

Our interview with Dr. Arthur E. Thomas, founder and director of the Center, follows.[3]

Art Thomas himself began to teach in an elementary school in Dayton in 1962. In his first school, in the center of the Black community, he found himself faced with a conflict between his impulse to "paddle" his "disruptive" students to keep order and his desire to become involved in the concerns and lives of his students. When three years later he had become an eighth grade teacher and a coach in track and football, he had given up paddling. "I refused to believe that my eighth graders could not learn and could not behave; the results were that they did learn and that they did behave." He had begun to reconsider other things too—and began helping his students to get scholarships, to get out of jail, to think about their own futures, and to begin to "love, trust, and respect" themselves. He also instituted a series of Black History Lectures, which he was allowed to conduct after school. In 1967, he was promoted to assistant principal of MacFarlane Elementary School, where for a year he attempted to create an environment in which students and their parents could learn and could establish an atmosphere of mutual trust with teachers.

In September, 1969, when the Dayton School System began to integrate its schools, Thomas was Director of the Model Cities Education Program. He and others from both the Black and white communities had warned that sudden integration in the racially tense city would be dangerous, but the school administration persisted in sending students from an all-Black urban community to an all-white Appalachian school. Severe trouble erupted at the school and one Black student was seriously hurt. On the next day, Thomas accompanied the Black students to school and attempted to help officials and parents keep order. Informed of the possibility of more violence, school officials promised to send a bus to take the Black students home. The bus did not arrive and tensions between Black and white students increased. Hoping to avoid more physical confrontations, Thomas persuaded the Black students to walk with him to safety in the administration building. When he returned to the school to collect a few Black students who still remained there, he was arrested—along with several of the Black students. Thomas left the jail only after all the Black students were released. He was subsequently fired by the Dayton Board of Education for "exceeding his authority."

Thomas decided to appeal the Board's decision and with the help of Dr. Ruth Burgin and three lawyers—the late Mr. Charles S. Bridge, Ms. Jean Camper Cahn and Dr. Edgar Cahn, he argued his case before administrative hearings. After three months of hearings, the Board of Education ruled against him.

No longer permitted to teach and work in the public school system of Dayton, Thomas began to consider alternative strategies for continuing his work with Black and poor children in the public schools. "The night the board ruled against me, we sat down and carefully analyzed my role; Dr. and Ms. Cahn kept reminding me that I had been an advocate for the children ever since the first day I had started teaching. Ms. Cahn, who had had long conferences with parents and students in the community, told me that the children perceived me as their advocate—someone who would stand behind them to defend their rights, no matter what. She said that no genuine advocate could work effectively from within the school system, that the system tends to mediate to the point where it co-opts all positions of advocacy, and that only in the legal system is it permissible to be an advocate. We decided on an O.E.O. legal services program led by an educator."

What has been the strategy behind the Center?

The Center was developed with several strategies in mind.

Our overall purpose was to educate students and parents about their human and constitutional rights as they relate to the institution called school.

This goal in itself might have led us in several directions, but we had one thing in particular that we had to deal with first. After the Dayton Board of Education and the school administration fired me, they wanted to prevent me from working with the students and parents. I was too effective from their point of view. School boards have a record of trying to eliminate teachers who seriously challenge them.

They kept trying to secure court orders to bar me from the children. Therefore we—all the parents and children and lawyers who were involved—decided that we needed a way for my skills and support to be useful to the community, even if I couldn't work directly in the system.

So we chose to develop the role of parent ombudsman who would be in continuous touch with the schools—the teachers, administration, counselors—and with the children and their families. Now the important thing to note about the way this strategy developed is that, though we started out from a simple need to replace me, we've ended up with a stronger, long range strategy. For one thing, while it is relatively easy to stop one individual, it is difficult to stop a growing number of informed, determined people.

Even more important, we now have begun a process through which we have our ten ombudsmen teaching others—parents and students—in the community. We're creating a ripple effect that will prepare many people to understand and deal effectively with the types of physical and psychological violence imposed upon the children by the school system and its agents. It's impossible for community people to have a lawyer with them whenever a child is injured. Our idea is to get the students and their parents to be their own lawyers—to help them have some control over their fate.

Another strategy was to make sure that the Center would be an independent institution. Students have learned the variety of forms of oppression that come down from the school system; one of the reasons they're beginning to trust us is because they know we stand completely apart from it.

As we work now, our lawyer develops legal tactics to deal with the inequities that are pointed out by me and our ombudsmen. What we're trying to do is to make the rights guaranteed by the Constitution real to and for children. The *Tinker* decision was important for this in theory—it said that your constitutional rights don't stop at the school door. We're trying to bridge the gap between theory and practice.

But how can you explain to students about their rights?

Many children seven years old, or nine years old, or fifteen years old, don't have any idea what basic rights are all about. They don't know what a Constitution is, or what a Declaration of Independence is. They don't have a conception of a right because the school teaches them that the only right they have when they walk into a school is to sit down and do as they are told. As the Cahns* point out, this situation affects the child's whole conception of what chance he or she has for fair play, for justice, for reciprocal relationships in the wider world. They, like Coleman, say that even the child's academic performance is influenced by his sense of whether he has any chance to control his own destiny.

When you start communicating to a young child or to a 16-year-old that he has certain basic rights, you're saying that he is human and that with that humanness comes real power for him to begin to have some control over his whole life. We tell him, "Look, you have certain basic constitutional rights. There are certain things that a teacher *can* do and *can't* do. We don't want you to react violently, we don't want you to use this information to start dehumanizing or destroying the teacher. But you do have certain control of your fate. Come to us and we will help you." Now he can begin to control what happens to him. He feels differently. Sometimes by teaching a student a basic right you get him into reading, sometimes you interest him in college, in medicine, in the law—you teach him to love, trust, and respect himself and his fellow man.

How then do you begin to help students implement their rights?

The first thing you do is teach them to love, trust, and respect themselves. Then you teach them to study the oppressor, the school, and its agents. For example, we start educating children and parents and teachers about the fact that words are sometimes used violently and that words sometimes result in a child's not wanting to learn, or in a child's not wanting to be anything, or in a child's not believing that he can be anything. They learn that the word thing has to be changed. Therefore we say that if you've been called dumb that is verbal abuse and there's an Ohio statute that protects you from verbal abuse. If you are suspended you are entitled to a hearing. You have the right to face your accusers. If you are not learning anything from eight o'clock in the morning until three o'clock in the afternoon then somebody has to be held accountable for the fact that you are not learning anything. *You* have a responsibility also—you have to get in there and try to learn. But if you are in that building from eight o'clock in the morning until three o'clock in the afternoon, and your teacher is forcing you to read a racist book that destroys your self-worth or that is not preparing you for the real world, you are

* All authors and works referred to in the text are cited in the bibliography.

not in school—you are in prison. It is a violation of the Constitution of the United States to incarcerate a person unless he has committed a crime.

We are going to have to institute various methods of accountability. I think you can deal with it very basically. No matter how bad his home conditions are, a child should know more at 3 o'clock in the afternoon than he knew at 8 o'clock in the morning. He should know more in June than he knew the preceding September, and he should certainly know more in 1972 than he knew in 1967. I think that the critical thing is that we have to stop assigning blame to the child. When we say, "The child is culturally deprived; the child is culturally disadvantaged," we are merely stereotyping a child; we are not blaming the institution. I am saying there is something wrong with the *school,* not the *child.*

As William Ryan says, we have to stop *Blaming the Victim.* A rapist is looked upon in this society very negatively. So is an embezzler, right? So is a murderer. So is a robber. But teachers who dehumanize? What about them? We are experts at making children the criminals, and adults and penal institutions, like schools, the saints. We hear people say, "The reason that the society is so messed up is because of the young." We've got to start assigning criminal names to criminals—and I'm not talking *only* about institutions because we've been doing that for too long. We say, "It is the school *system,"* and that is correct.—the oppression *is* systemic. But how do you identify who's wrong *within* an institution? From the child's perspective, it is the principal or the teacher who is destroying him or her, not the system.

Let me give you a very specific example of how this thing operates. A second grader was going around a school with the zipper down on his pants. Now the principal said that the child, a second grader, had "deviant sexual behavior." Now, a little research showed that his mother was on welfare, and his mother did not have enough money to buy him some pants, or even to buy him a zipper. She was trying to feed him. And the reason that he was in school was because his mother had impressed upon him the need to go to school every day so that he could *be somebody,* so that he could make some money. Therefore he was in school and he did not have a zipper on his pants. The principal sent him home and said that he was going around exposing himself and that that was deviant sexual behavior. The principal had no basic concept of what it was like to be poor. He did not have sense enough to ask the child if he had another pair of pants at home. That kind of behavior, in my opinion, means that the principal is guilty of *misfeasance, malfeasance,* and *incompetence.* What we're saying is those kinds of acts of atrocity have to be eliminated. Potentially, that child could be the doctor with the cure for cancer. Teachers who see his office card marked "deviant," however, will treat him like a criminal, not like a future M.D.

How does your work at the Center attempt to deal with examples like this?

When we can develop a strategy whereby teachers and administrators are held criminally responsible for the kinds of atrocities they are guilty of creating and implementing in the public schools, then we'll get to protecting that child's right to an education. What we're trying to develop is a legal strategy for actually documenting and charging that teacher or principal or administrator with being an accessory to whatever crime the child commits in later life as a result of a teacher's or administrator's cruelty. Lawyers will always say, "Why, that's ridiculous." Many lawyers have been programmed into thinking a certain way, too. But I see no basic difference between a warden in a prison and a principal. There are psychological dimensions of violence and I think that the law and lawyers and the courts have got to redefine violence.

It's violent to dehumanize a person. You can be very violent with words. You can be very violent with nonverbal types of communication. To refuse to touch a child is a form of violence. We have a case in our files where a teacher was a very effective teacher in terms of teaching the skills—reading, writing, arithmetic, etc.—and that's hard to find today. But she was getting no results with fourth graders because every morning she went into the room and sprayed disinfectant. She was just a clean teacher who liked everything to be perfect and she was very methodical. But the point is, the children perceived that as being a negative thing and they perceived that she felt that they were dirty and that she was much better than them. Therefore they responded to her negatively. Our staff is working with her now. She put the disinfectant can down and she's working a lot more effectively with the children.

Then you don't always go to court with the problem?

No. Our strategies have to be flexible. The most important thing is for us to communicate effectively to the oppressed what their rights are. The only way that we're really going to have the kind of impact we need is for everybody to have the same kind of information so that they can start affecting what happens to them.

Knowledge is power—so when a nine-year-old or an eleven-

Student governments should have real, as opposed to symbolic, power to make the vital decisions that affect the lives of students in the school—curriculum, discipline, etc.

—Recommended by an individual student from the Student Board of Inquiry into High School Discipline.

year-old comes to me and says, "I'm tired of that teacher yelling at me. Next time she does it, I'm going to knock her down," I say, "Listen. The next time that teacher is mean to you, be cool. Just sit there in the classroom and don't say anything for 20 minutes. Then, when you are completely calm and in control, raise your hand. When she calls on you, tell her coolly and calmly, "Ms. Jones, what you did a few minutes ago, the way you talked to me, has psychologically dehumanized me, has made me feel like an animal, like a stupid animal. If that happens often enough, a child like me grows up thinking of himself as stupid and ugly and he can never function as a human being again. So unless you refrain from treating me in such a manner, I may have no alternative but to take you to the U.S. District Court and explain all this to the judge. And let me remind you, Ms. Jones, that there is a good possibility that I can win a $100,000 damage suit against you if I charge you with a 'psychological tort.' "

We work on this statement and practice it just like practicing for the Christmas play. We've tried this. It works. The child develops a new sense of power and fate-control. The teacher develops a new sense of responsibility relative to her behavior.

This is quite a different consequence from what usually happens. When Ms. Jones hollers at him, his immediate reaction is to holler back at her, or Ms. Jones hollers at him, and his immediate reaction is to put his head down and turn off everything that has happened, or Ms. Jones hollers at him, and he internalizes it and goes out on the playground and slaps another student and then gets into trouble in another way. Then Ms. Jones, the oppressor, has won, and there is no way of letting her know that she may have started an armed robbery that will occur in two years or five years or that she may have contributed to that child's graduation to Attica or San Quentin, or dope or welfare or psychological death.

Imagine the impact we could have if we could show this kind of example on television or film or even on recordings. We could get to the students—and maybe even the teachers.

I'm trying to work on other examples of using the law—like taking a tort, and phrasing it in a way that a young child, a second grader, can understand. So that he can then start explaining these things to the teacher. I strongly believe that one of the basic problems is that teachers do not understand children. Teachers do not understand the child's perception and only a child can teach the teacher how he feels and in that way change the teacher's behavior towards that child.

Let me give you another example of how we try to teach law to the brothers and sisters as a tool to protect them. An eighteen-year-old brother came into our office last year and said, "Look, Art, that jive teacher keeps messing with me and I am going to knock him down if he doesn't get off my back."

I said, "Dig, Brother, if you hit the teacher he can sue you for assault and battery and he might be able to have you arrested." I said, "Why don't you just lay back and be cool, and let him hit you and when and if he does, don't hit him back —just get your witnesses together and then you can sue *him.*"

He came into our office one day. He was smiling and he said, "Hey, Art, you are a jive cat. I waited all year for that dude to hit me and he didn't hit me and I was planning on suing the dude so I could use the money to buy me a short [car]." He is in college now—so you can see that our approach is useful in many different ways.

Of course another effective way to deal with the problem is to take those individuals responsible for racism, dehumanization, and oppression to the courts or to the public and hold them accountable for their atrocities against children. We do not need to look for scapegoats in the poor Black community or the poor white community, or the Indian community, or the Puerto Rican community or the youth community. The policy makers and the administrators of that policy must be held accountable.

It sounds as though you're relying on criminal statutes and law. Why not bring civil cases?

First of all, we're exploring the civil statutes as well. We aren't counting on one thing to be the panacea. One reason why criminal suits are appealing is that district attorneys and county prosecutors are political creatures. You have about fifty registered voters down swearing out a warrant charging a teacher with something like criminal neglect of a child—then the D.A. sees perhaps a sensational case that will enable him to advance his political future. The other thing to remember is he is not about to reject the desires of fifty or sixty or a hundred registered voters. Also, don't forget, criminal cases can be brought without money—a poor mother can bring a case. All she has to do is swear out a warrant.

But suppose you don't win in court?

But, look, I'm dealing with another thing. Even if the case doesn't get one inch in a courtroom, what we're doing is re-defining what a criminal is. It's not the child who is the criminal—it's the teacher or administrator who destroys the child's humanness that is the criminal. The word game is very important. By assigning criminal definitions to what so-called educators are doing, I'm trying to get both the oppressed and the oppressor to see that certain acts committed by school people are criminal.

But won't you have to prove premeditation—and isn't that a hard thing to prove?

Yes. This idea is a very radical, even unsound strategy, as the law is now used. But I'm saying that there is premeditation. Black and poor children are being deliberately destroyed so that they cannot compete with middle class and rich white children for jobs.

I'm also saying that this country has a habit of responding very quickly in some situations and responding very slowly in others. For example, as a result of the rebellions that occurred in the 60's and 70's, many state governments and the federal government moved swiftly to pass legislation that dealt with restricting the right to freedom of assembly, interstate travel, etc. A great deal of this legislation dealt with limiting the young or protecting institutions from the young, the poor, the Black—the oppressed.

If it was logical to deal with a crisis situation in order to preserve institutions in the manner I just described, then is it not logical to deal with the physical and psychological destruction of children, which in my opinion is in the crisis stage, by redefining our concepts of who the criminals really are and what the consequences of criminal actions are relative to the survival of our children?

Furthermore, at no time in the near future will all oppressed children be able to have their own lawyers. Therefore, it is very important that we find ways to communicate to children and their parents that *they* are not the criminals. If we do not do this, the self-fulfilling prophecy will once again force them to act like criminals and later to become criminals. On the other hand, we have to develop a strategy to protect their right not to be destroyed. We have tried everything from money to sensitivity sessions to in-service training for teachers to performance contracts to get accountability. Why not try criminal statutes? Teachers are not doing children a *favor* if they teach them effectively and treat them as human beings—that's their *job*. We have tried moral persuasion already, and it hasn't worked well. But nobody wants to be fined or to go to jail.

We have to develop strategies for massive attitudinal

Distribution of printed materials in school should not be restricted except when the literature incites the reader to physical violence by instructing him to do something which will physically harm someone else. Although the principal should not censor in-school publications or restrict the distribution of outside material within the school building, he should receive a copy of any material distributed in the school, not for his approval but for his information. As far as a principal trying to suppress petitions or Inflammatory literature in his building, it's a waste of time . . . the ideas will be inside the building anyway. . . .

—Recommendation from the Dayton Student Board of Inquiry into High School Discipline.

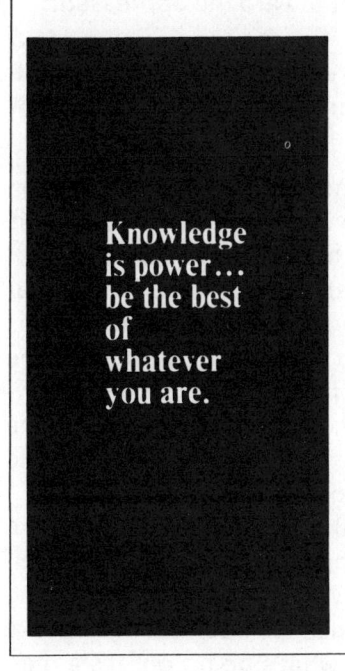

Knowledge is power... be the best of whatever you are.

Student Rights Handbook
for Dayton, Ohio

1. SCHOOL DISCIPLINE
2. STUDENT EXPRESSION
3. COUNSELING
4. PHYSICAL PUNISHMENT
5. POLICE IN THE SCHOOLS
6. MARRIAGE AND PREGNANCY
7. VERBAL ABUSE OF STUDENTS
8. RIGHT TO AN EDUCATION
9. ARRESTS
10. CONCLUSION

In any event, a student-mother, whether married or unmarried, may return to her regular school in her regular program in the semester following the birth of her child. No student may be excluded from the regular day school program because she is a mother.

7
Verbal Abuse Of Students

Some teachers and school officials insist upon calling students "dumb," or other derogatory terms. This must be stopped. Students have the right to be free from the psychological damage which comes from verbal abuse. "Dumb," for example, should be applied only to those students who lack the power of speech, and then not in a derogatory manner.

When a teacher calls a student "dumb," or any other dehumanizing word, the student should immediately make a complaint to the principal, as well as inform his parents of the incident. If the principal does not act upon the matter (at a minimum, an apology would be appropriate) the complaint should then be brought to the attention of the superintendent's office or the Board of Education. If no action is taken at this level, or if the verbal abuse continues, the student should contact an attorney or the Student Rights Center (223-8228) to consider further action.

Further, the provisions of Sections 2901.20, and 2901.21 of the Ohio Code may be applicable. Section 2901.20 provides that no student or person in attendance at a school shall engage in hazing or commit an act which injures, degrades, or disgraces a fellow student or person attending such school. Violators may be fined up to $200.00, or imprisoned up to six months, or both. Section 2901.21 provides that no teacher or other person in charge of a school shall knowingly permit hazing or attempts to haze, frighten, degrade, or disgrace a person attending such school. Violators may be fined up to $100.00.

8
Right To An Education

Every student has the constitutional right to an education. As the Supreme Court of the United States has stated, "Where the state has undertaken to provide it (an education), (it) is a *right* which must be available to all on equal terms." (Emphasis added.) *Brown* v. *Board of Education*, 347 U.S. 483, 493 (1954). The dimensions of this right are still unclear. However students, as the consumers of education, should demand that the education to which they have a right be a reality.

The Dayton Board of Education has made a general statement on student involvement in educational policy. "Students should have a voice in the formulation of school policies and decisions which affect their education and lives as students. Through such participation, students can be a powerful resource for the improvement of the school, the educational system and the community." Students should accept the Board's challenge.

change. The oppressed have to change their attitudes and behavior toward self and the oppressor. The oppressors have to change their attitudes and behavior toward the oppressed.

So part of the strategy is that you're redefining who the criminal is. Are you also redefining who the defenders of the law should be?

Yes. Chief Justice Burger and others in the legal profession are talking about the fact that the administration of justice is reaching a crisis stage because of tremendous case loads, administrative problems, new regulations, etc. Jean and Edgar Cahn have stated that there are many things that citizens or trained technicians can do to take the pressure off the courts and to enhance the possibility of more people receiving justice. Like Thomas Jefferson said (even though he wasn't talking about Black people), educate the masses and tyranny and oppression will disappear!

What we are trying to do is to take mothers on welfare, take young students and provide the opportunity for them to develop their own survival strategies. We are trying to get young students who understand the kinds of oppression that are going on to teach the community what's going on. It's a matter of teaching, it's a matter of effective communication.

It's a matter of the so-called professional learning from the people as well as teaching the people. It's a matter of loving, trusting, and respecting the people and it's a matter of doing *with* rather than doing *for* the people.

It's also a matter of winning.

For example, our parents go to school hearings and talk to principals, and they point out to the principal that he's wrong on this and wrong on that.

Our parents are learning how not to be manipulated by the principal. The principal will almost always try to convince the parents that he has the most difficult job in the world. Then he'll go back to what this child's brother did, and what the child's mother and father did, and what his grandmother's mother did to point out that they've given the child every possible chance.

We are trying to get our ombudsmen to orient themselves thoroughly to how some principals and teachers lie and deliberately deceive people. We want parents to always move from a *child advocacy* perspective. The principals and teachers have associations to protect their rights. This is a society of checks and balances, so children should also have an ascociation to protect their rights. We hope that the parent ombudsmen check the "new sovereign immunity" that the "public servant" has over the child, the parents, and the community.

So the ombudsmen are the real link with the community?

Yes, but not just that. Because the ombudsmen are deeply involved, sometimes they come up with the most important legal points, just as some of the best criminal reform law has come from prisoners and not the dudes that sit in the big law firms. The jailhouse lawyer type dudes are living what's going on—not reading about it. For example, Ms. Robinson, one of our ombudsmen, is a state chairman of the Welfare Rights Organization (NWRO). She's been working with me for quite some time—since way back in '62. The only way we could get results then was to picket, shout at, and threaten the oppressor. Now by sitting in sessions with the lawyers, analyzing school law, and studying the oppressor, she and other ombudsmen have developed other strategies for dealing with the establishment. Let me give you an example—it wasn't our lawyer but Ms. Robinson who read the school code, the Ohio State Statute as it related to school expulsions. She said, "Look, this thing says that if a child is expelled, he has a right to a hearing." When one of her children was expelled she pointed out the rule to our lawyer. The Center is probably one of the few places where the oppressed can go and read law books. You usually have to be a lawyer to get into the law library downtown. Many of our people don't have access to or know how to use the library. But at the Center we have law books right in the community and people come in and read those books. So Ms. Robinson read the book and it said, "If a child is expelled, he is entitled to a hearing."

Now, let me tell you what the school administration's strategy was. Whenever a child was expelled, the assistant superintendent in charge of pupil personnel would send out a copy of the part of the regulation which dealt with his right to expel a child. But he did not send out the section of the regulation which dealt with the child's right to a hearing before the Board of Education. As a result of Ms. Robinson's discovery, the staff attorney asked for a hearing before the Board of Education. The Board of Education held the hearing and the Board of Education directed the assistant superintendent in charge of pupil personnel to review its expulsion policy. There had been a number of expulsions from the Dayton School system in the previous eighteen months and the Board of Education sensed that the Student Rights Center could very easily bring *every* child that had been expelled in for a a hearing before the Board of Education. That would take a lot of time and effort and energy on the part of the school board and administrators.

They don't expel many students any more. Now what they do is suspend them. They always change their strategy—and so will we. That's another reason that we have to be very careful—as you get freedoms for the young brothers and sisters, the administrators and teachers find other ways, maybe more subtle ways, to oppress them.

Why do you think they concentrate so much on getting the children out of school?

Some of it is just overt racism. Some of it is institutionalized racism. Subconsciously they feel, "Dirty nigger, I don't want you in here anyway. So get out." That's what it boils down to. Other reasons are connected to administrative convenience. Some administrators don't necessarily hate children, but they see children as inconveniences. They see a child who is mistreating another child as a problem who has to be sent home so they can do their quarterly reports. Or they see a child who cuts a class as somebody that is walking around the hall that should be sent home so that he won't pull the fire alarm. I'm convinced, I'm totally convinced that if you explain to a child the reason why you want him to do something, he will respond positively.

But most administrators don't feel that they have any obligation to explain anything to a student. They don't treat students as consumers or customers; they treat them as criminals or as prisoners of war or as the enemy.

The child who is extorting money from another child did not have that ability to extort when he came out of his mother's womb. It was obviously taught by someone. It was probably taught by an adult. But do the teachers attempt to deal with the problem of extortion? Hell, no! They're too busy dealing with Columbus discovering something that some Indian brothers had already inhabited, and telling lies about Abraham Lincoln freeing us when he really pawned us. Now wouldn't it be more practical, in terms of the seriousness of conflict situations in our society, for a teacher to deal effectively with the problem of mistreating one's fellow man? But the reality of it is that teachers do not know *how* to deal with those things.

In not dealing with the problem the teacher implicitly contributes to it. The teacher has no information or strategy or knowledge whatsoever in solving the problem of extortion. She sends the child home so he can then go to another school on the way home to extort from another child. Rather than teaching this child that it is important that he learn to love, trust, and respect the other child, she sends him home. Instead of sending the child home she could go through a thing like "Stand up here, Johnny. Now, three of you go up and take Johnny's money. Just take Johnny's money from him. Now, how do you feel about that, Johnny?" That doesn't happen. That never happens.

No programs are developed to teach the young brothers and sisters how to relate to each other. No. Because it's very simple for teachers to open that one textbook, say "Read Chapters 3 and 4," and that's it. Sit down and be a good *boy* and you can pass—stand up and try to be a *man* and you get kicked out.

What we are doing is attempting to develop an entire society of robots. But a society of robots or yes-men doesn't correspond with our stated objective of democracy. As Barbara Sizemore says in her testimony before the Mondale Committee, if we don't get about the business of establishing systems for participatory democracy in institutions that socialize our children for a so-called democracy, there will be little chance for having a real democracy.

Ermon O. Hogan has written in *Racial Crisis in American Education,* "Although our schools have provided a quasi-common heritage, they have not provided a common experience out of which youth could learn to develop the responsibilities of freedom, to respect universal equality, and to acquire the skills necessary to guarantee prosperity through the years to come."

Some students are learning, though. They are learning that teachers make mistakes, they are learning that administrators lie, they are learning that some of our institutions are oppressive. They are responding by trying to free themselves so that they can free others, so we can build a free society.

I believe that some children condition themselves to take out the anger and frustration that they feel toward a teacher or an administrator or a parent on other children rather than the adult. Experience has taught them that they will lose in a confrontation with an adult. Children, like any oppressed group, sometimes behave like the oppressor. Any individual who is being oppressed has developed a way to get back at something or someone. If he doesn't, he may easily lose his sanity.

The child learns that the principal is always right, even when the child knows that he is wrong. The child knows that the principal will always say that the teacher is right even when the child knows that the teacher is wrong. And often the child's parents will make the same assumption.

Why would the parents tend to assume that the child is always wrong?

Parents are sometimes very repressive. In fact they are in many respects just as repressive as teachers. They don't do this intentionally—it's because they see education as the one thing that can improve the conditions in life for their children. They want their children to do well in life so they see the school, the teacher, the principal as a ray of hope and a way out of slavery and oppression. Because his parents will not accept the fact that it's *possible* that a teacher might be wrong, the child will get very up-tight because he says, "Where else can I go—I ask my mother and father to listen to me and trust me and they won't. I can't deal with the school alone." So often the results are a gang or possibly some drugs, or a robbery and eventually a cell in Attica or San Quentin. And whenever the parents have to come to the principal's office, they get a game put on them. The warden always asks them, "What about your child's responsibility? Look at the thing objectively." And when they run

Student courts should handle all disciplinary cases in the school. . . . Student judges should be elected by the student body. A set of rules should be formulated by student committees, then voted on by the entire student body. Students could function as attorneys in student court. Students could make sure other students followed the directions of the court. The emphasis should be on corrective, rather than punitive, measures. If a child is acting up in class because he's a slow reader, for example, students could be assigned to tutor that child intensively until he catches up.

—Recommendation from the Dayton Student Board of Inquiry into High School Discipline.

that on a parent, what they're really saying is, "Accept my point of view."

How are you dealing with this?

The biggest job is getting adults to look at children as human beings who have rights. We don't have our lawyer running to court every day because we think it's more important to have him explaining the law to parents. Parents respect lawyers, and teachers, and preachers. The lawyer's real job is to give the parents backbone and insight. The parents can say, "We've got our lawyer—he can lay some information on us and then we can deal." So the lawyer's there, backing them up, giving them information.

Remember, a lot of violence occurs in the Black community—folks are scared. So when the Man talks about law and order and responsibilities, Black folks listen and poor folks listen. There is a tendency for people to speak the same words—the words of the oppressor—back to us at the Center and say, when we start talking about the rights of children, "What about their *responsibilities*? Why are you helping the hoodlums?" They have trouble seeing that a child, when he has been in trouble, deserves legal representation.

So we have to remind them first that they don't get upset about a murderer or a rapist having a lawyer. Why should they think that we're protecting criminals when all we're saying is that a child, even though he may be wrong, has a right to be represented? Or even though he may be wrong in terms of his actions, we have to deal with the reason for his actions. Why should they get upset when a child who misunderstands and therefore gets into trouble has someone to represent him? I'm saying you have to develop within the community a new appreciation for the fact that children are oppressed and you have to show the community that if a child does something, he does something for a reason. You have to get the community out of the whole scapegoat syndrome, where they automatically start blaming children for atrocities that adults are responsible for.

So the ombudsmen really have to educate the community in a new way to see how the schools treat children?

The ombudsmen spend most of their time working with individual students and parents. For example, if a child is suspended, the ombudsman calls up the principal, and asks him why the child was suspended. Just the fact that an ombudsman calls up a principal and questions the fact that he has suspended a child changes that principal's behavior. Just the fact that the Student Rights Center exists changes teachers' and administrators' behavior. For example, just before school opened last September we worked with a local newspaper reporter, explaining the negative aspects of corporal punishment. The reporter then wrote a full-page article on corporal punishment. Many teachers told me that they are now apprehensive about paddling children because now they know what the state statute is on corporal punishment. Many parents read the article and said, "The next time my child is mistreated I'm going to do something about it." If we had merely taken it to court, it would have been a legal exercise between two lawyers and a judge.

The fact that students have rights has simply never occurred to many people—and that's rich people and poor people, Black people and white people. We don't even see a child in the context of "rights." We see a child in the context of somebody whom you tell what to do, and somebody who is supposed to do as he or she is told.

When the parents do catch on, it must really help their children.

Yes, it does. Alvin Poussaint, the Black psychiatrist, pointed this out in an article in *Ebony* magazine when he said that the Ocean-Hill-Brownsville incident was one of the best things that had ever happened in education because, oppressed, Black children saw their parents going up against police officers and the system for them to have the right to go to school. A Black child—standing outside one of those schools in Ocean-Hill-Brownsville watching his mother and watching his father confront policemen—started getting things going around in his head about the importance of school and about the need for him to go to school. And he started learning with a new kind of enthusiasm because his mother and his father went in there and fought for him to have that right to go to school. School for those children became an important part of life, not just a prison they were forced into.

The Center's parent ombudsmen include parents who have been on welfare, and parents who have a fair income. There are Black and white ombudsmen who work with Black and white families. When the children see the ombudsmen confronting the system on their behalf, the children show a new desire and have new hope. The ombudsmen help the children develop a positive attitude. The children begin to believe that they are not always wrong and that they have some degree of fate control.

I'm saying that children—like Blacks—like Chicanos—like Puerto Ricans—like Indians—like women—are recognizing that they are human beings as a result of the fact that some of us have been telling them that they are. "You're beautiful, you have a right to this, you have a right to that." If you keep telling somebody that they're good or that they can control what happens to them, then they start believing it and doing it.

While I was assistant principal at MacFarlane School, I used to ask the young Black men to stand up and clap for the young Black women in the school. I still use this method to impress upon young Black men at an early age—like 3 years old—that they should love, trust, and respect Black women. Black men must not fall into the trap set by racist social theorists like Daniel P. Moynihan. Moynihan asserted that Black society is dominated by Black women. He called Black society a matriarchy, and left the impression that Black men must seek to dominate Black women. Dr. Jacquelyne J. Jackson pointed out in a recent issue of *Ebony* magazine that part of Moynihan's thesis was dead wrong: one of the reasons, she said, that more Black women head households is not that they are domineering, but that there simply have not been enough Black men to go around.

Because they have accepted Moynihan's racist thesis, some Black men have seen strong Black women as a threat to their manhood. This is a tragic waste. Black men should not try to prove their manhood by trying to destroy the strength of Black womanhood. The future of Black people depends, not on Black men dominating Black women, but on cementing their partnership with them. We must revere the courage and brilliance of our women and support and join their actions toward effecting Black liberation.

To get back to the issue of student rights, things like the Students Rights Handbook help too. We've tried to get those books out into the community. The young brothers and sisters walk through the school hall. The teacher says, "Shut up, Johnny." Johnny gets the book out and says, "Hey, man, I can't read this thing. Look in here and see what it says I should do when the teacher hollers at me." So a student who can read reads to him about what he can do about the verbal abuse of a student. Johnny raps to the teacher about Section 2901.20 and 2901.21 of the Ohio Code, and the teacher gets off his back.

But what about the abuse—physical or verbal—of the teacher?

Usually you find that when a child hits a teacher, the teacher has passed the first lick. We're trying to explode the myth about George Washington and teachers and principals never telling a lie. Let me give you another example of how the ombudsmen work. A student came to the Center who had been suspended twelve times. So a student ombudsman worked with him. The student ombudsman's name is James Phillips. James said, "Look, man, what are you going to do when you go back to school?" "I'm going to make sure that the cat doesn't hit me again." "What are you going to do if he hits you?" "I'm going to try to knock his head off." So James said, "Look, man, you've been out of school twelve times for fighting. And you're talking about going back to fighting. Now, isn't it obvious to you that the man, the principal, is running games on you? And what can you do to make sure that you and this cat don't fight but at the same time you can get something out of school, 'cause you're just wasting a lot of time and risking getting yourself ripped off. Do you understand that, man?" One of the reasons the student understood was that James is the same age as he is. So he says, "Yeah, I guess so." So then he and James sat down and they developed a strategy to get five students together so that they could work with each other to protect themselves from the principal and from the teachers of the school.

Have you thought about sending in teams of lawyers?

The one thing that I recognize about a law and order society, about the way we've been trained and programmed, is that we only respond when we become personally involved. Most lawyers analyze the problem. They take the problem through ninety-nine research steps, and they think that they then have all the answers. I'm saying that a mother who has seen her child victimized, a mother who has in fact been victimized herself, feels a lot more compassion. A mother can't go home at five and say, "Well, we'll finish this tomorrow." She stays there until six or seven or eight in the evening until that problem is solved. The other thing is that she's a part of that community. Many of our cases come to our ombudsmen at home, not to the Center. A child with his parent will call up one of the ombudsmen at home, or go knock on the door, and say, "Look, Ms. Wiley, they're doing this to us—what can we do?" And they sit down right there in the home and solve the problem.

Because that ombudsman is in the community, because that ombudsman has come through the whole Civil Rights struggle, because the ombudsman knows and understands the child, because the ombudsman knows the principal and teachers and the kinds of games they run, the ombudsman can relate and deal effectively with the problem. Another important thing is that parents don't feel that they have to speak perfect grammar to be able to talk to the ombudsman about the problem. The ombudsman gets a lot of information, a lot more insight, into the problem, I think, than a so-called professional would. We try to work with the ombudsmen on certain interview techniques. We try to teach the ombudsmen about the importance of confidentiality and follow-up. But I'm saying that the ombudsman is a very emotional, intricate part of that community and the ombudsman responds to clients like human beings rather than like rats running through mazes, which is what most professionals—lawyers, social workers, teachers, administrators, doctors, judges, —tend to do.

Is it possible for the legal profession to be deprofessionalized?

Let me answer this way. We are developing a model statute for due process which we will present to the Board of Education and I think that it might work like this: a student is suspended, let's say, for hollering at his teacher. And let's say that we have not necessarily an ombudsman, but maybe one of the women from the League of Women Voters who's hearing the case. Well, the first thing that would be different is that the teacher would have to state why she kicked the student out of school. And then the child would have an opportunity to respond to the teacher's charges. Then the principal would be asked in what kinds of detail he investigated the case prior to the time that he sent the child home. Then the mother would probably be asked, "Has the child had problems with other teachers?" And the child would be asked how he feels about the whole thing. So it's quite possible that in that whole process the child has to take a look at himself or herself, the parent has to take a look at himself or herself, the teacher has to take a look at himself or herself, and the principal has to take a look at himself or herself.

Yes, it is possible for the legal profession to deprofessionalize, but it is also possible for everybody to have access to the strategies used now by the legal profession mainly to protect the rich and the powerful.

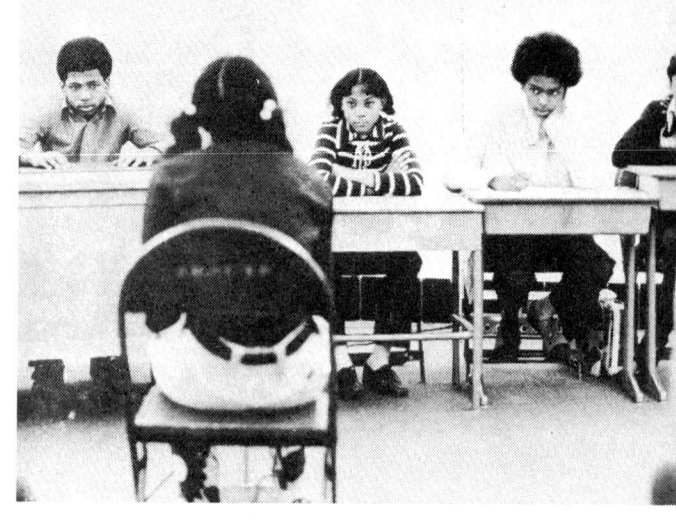

What's your feeling about para-professionals and auxiliary personnel of that sort?

I think that some of the best guidance counselors are students—students who don't have Master's degrees in guidance. They sit down and they say, "Look, man, you don't need to do it like that, you need to do it like this."

Frank Riessman, at the 1969 Career Opportunities Conference in Denver, pointed out that of 1000 federal programs that they examined, students in 23 of those programs showed noticeable gains in cognitive achievement. And out of the twenty-three programs where students showed noticeable gains, eleven of them were programs that involved para-professionals. So maybe we should pay students and parents to teach, and let the teachers who are ineffective seek employment elsewhere.

When I directed the Model Cities Education program we had an excellent program where Black and white Vietnam war veterans worked as teacher aides at the second grade level. They were working toward degrees in education. Some have already finished. They had excellent rapport with the students. They also greatly influenced the attitudes and behavior of the teachers. I think all auxiliary type jobs should enable folks to develop to the very maximum of their potential and not lock them in so that they can advance only so much. One of the veterans in our program is now working on his Ph.D.

But if you want to affect all the children in the country, don't you have to deal with the professionalization in the schools?

Yes. Teacher organizations in my opinion are mainly concerned with making as much money as possible for doing as little work as possible.

One way to deal with the so-called professional is to simply wipe out compulsory attendance. I agree with Edgar Friedenberg that compulsory attendance as it exists today functions as a Bill of Attainder. We have to develop the kind of learning atmosphere where the child learns to love, trust, and respect himself and his peers and others, and to develop skills that will enable him to survive as a human being and to develop to the very maximum of his or her potential. My first inclination is to wipe out compulsory attendance, but at the same time I want to make sure that we develop some kind of mechanisms that will protect children and maximize their life chances.

On the other hand I have very serious problems with de-schooling, as Ivan Illich calls it, because it doesn't, in my opinion, adequately deal with the question of institutionalized racism. If you're going to have a de-schooled society run by the racist oppressors who are running this one, then

I'm opposed to it. At the same time I see great benefits in developing very special skills in a period of six weeks and not keeping people off the job market by insisting that they go through a number of worthless exercises to be certified. I don't see any magic about going to a building every day, and I believe students learn by doing, not by listening to a teacher who may or may not know what he or she is talking about.

It's hard to decide about programs and changes that look good on the surface. For example, even if Head Start is in many respects a good program, the positive aspects seem to get wiped out anyway. When I consider something like de-schooling, I have to wonder what will happen to the children who are catching hell now. One of the things that I recognize is that, as a result of the whole Civil Rights movement of the 1960's, Black teachers have become a lot more aware. Despite the fact that there's a tremendous amount of pressure being exerted on them to make sure that Black children are not taught properly, Black teachers are beginning to take care of business just the same. As Black children become more aware and start becoming more knowledgeable, all of a sudden we hear talk about reading not being important and arithmetic not being important, and de-emphasizing schooling and de-schooling.

It's the same thing with some white "educators" telling us what is *good* for the Black child. White teachers have developed missionary strategies for slavery 1960-1970 style. When I was directing the Model Cities Education program, I visited a kindergarten class and the children were taking a nap. They got there about eight. They took a nap at 8:45, a nap about 10:30, and another nap at 11:30 and they went home at twelve. I asked the teacher what was going on. She said, "Well, you have to let *these* children develop at their own leisure because you can't psychologically frustrate them." My response to her was, "Well, when these same children get to the third grade and put their heads on the desk and start taking naps because they can't read or because they are in the habit of sleeping all day they will have been taught to sleep and waste time by you. You will be responsible for their being suspended or expelled. Now it seems to me that those who are behind in a race 'must forever remain behind or run faster than the man in front.' So what I want you to do is to get those damn blocks out of the way, stop those half-day naps and siestas and start teaching them to read, write, and do arithmetic. If you push them and they learn, at least they will be able to get a job and afford a psychiatrist. If you go at the rate that you're going and they learn absolutely nothing, then they won't be able to get a job and they won't know anything and at the same time they'll be mixed up and confused because they won't be able to compete in society." The point I'm making is that's another form of racism. Many white teachers assume Black children can't learn and so they let them sleep, play basketball, or not come to class.

As things are now I agree with Mario Fantini and Donald Harris: we have to provide as many alternatives as possible and we have to stop looking for a panacea. The only thing that could be worse than what we have now would be Hitler's concentration camps, and I believe that they are on the way, American style.

Do you have the same kind of mixed feelings about the voucher system or alternative schools?

The voucher system points up another legal point I'd like to deal with—the whole business of school systems functioning as monopolies. One of the reasons the school systems are so ineffective is that they have no competition. One of the things I liked about vouchers is that they have the potential to destroy the monopoly of the public school system. What other alternative does the poor child have? We need competitive models, we need community-controlled schools, we need free schools, university-run schools, welfare-rights-run schools, schools run by militant organizations, voucher schools, etc.

There *are* good educational models for Black children. Imamu Imiri Baraka has a good model; Elijah Muhammad has a good model; the Roxbury Free Schools in Boston, Harlem Prep, and the Nairobi Schools in California are good models. The voucher system, if not controlled by the oppressor, *could* make it possible to expand these models.

But the critical issue that has to be dealt with is a redistribution of power. Poor folks need power and money to operate different kinds of schools.

Committees composed of parents and students should interview prospective teachers. This should be done on an individual school, rather than a system-wide, basis. The students and parents could ask the teacher questions based on the needs of the school. This is especially needed when race is a real factor—for example, when white teachers apply to predominantly Black schools. This committee arrangement would not inhibit racial integration, but would make teacher selection more intelligent and more democratic. It would also give the particular school's community a direct say about its teachers.

—Recommendation from the Dayton Student Board of Inquiry into High School Discipline.

As for alternatives to the schools, there are a couple of questions to be dealt with. One is that the big oppressive institution called the school system is responsible for educating our children. So what you're doing if you start a free school, even though *that* free school may have the interest of the children at heart, is relieving the public school of its responsibility. The over-all strategy should be to stay on their cases and make sure they educate the children as they should be educated. But if there were enough alternatives, the school system would be forced either to produce or become obsolete, I would support the alternatives.

Are you saying that if the school system were doing its job right, alternatives wouldn't be necessary?

Schools *are* doing their job though. In fact, the schools in urban communities are doing *precisely* what they're designed to do. They are designed to transmit the cultural heritage. The cultural heritage in this country is one of racism. Urban schools are designed to make sure that you always have busboys, dishwashers, and folks for white people to look down upon psychologically.

The superintendent is paid to be sure that Black children do not learn because the system does not want Black children to be in a position to compete with white children for jobs. It's a perpetuation of the class structure in this country.

Schools are also designed to make sure that banks keep getting money placed into those banks by teachers. You see 85% of the schools' budget goes into salaries. And they're designed for the wax companies to sell wax, for the toilet paper companies to sell toilet paper, and for the food companies to sell food. Schools are a 61 billion dollar a year business. Poor children are used as tools for that business.

The role of the education lobby, and its self-interest in any educational expenditures, cannot be overlooked. For instance, the Southwest Region of the Ohio Education Association gave an appreciation dinner for members of the state legislature who voted for the latest school appropriations bill in the state legislature. Had any other interest group done this for their legislative benefactors, there would have been a public outcry. Not so with the educators.

As of January, 1972, some 28 suits in 18 states, all modeled on *Serrano*, had been filed. It is being discovered, however, that in state after state, urban schools will receive less money per pupil in any plan proposed for equalization of per pupil expenditures. Also, the Ohio Education Association is the plaintiff in the Ohio suit modeled on *Serrano*. Their legal fees, as in all these cases, are very high. So is the OEA's self-interest. To equalize per pupil expenditures across the state would of necessity increase the teacher salaries across the state.

Do you think the busing will make any difference to this system?

As Lerone Bennett points out in *The Challenge of Blackness*, integration and separation should be looked upon as strategies for liberation. I am opposed to any strategy that is going to damage children—psychologically or physically. It really amazes me how we have such little regard for the rights of children and how in most instances we have such little regard for the abilities of children and yet on the question of integration we ask *them* to deal effectively with the problem that *we* have not effectively dealt with ourselves.

If we can put them on buses at age seven to deal with institutionalized racism—why can't we put them in voting booths at age seven to vote on whether or not they want to be bused? It's easy for us to say how we feel about it, but then *we* are not being bused. Why can't children be elected to the Board of Education at age seven? Are 7-year-olds or 14-year-olds or 16-year-olds represented by or judged by their peers in our society? I think we should be asking the students how they feel about it.

As I stated at the Conference on Education for Blacks sponsored by the Congressional Black Caucus, I seriously doubt the utility of busing to improve the education of Black students. "Racial balance" and "desegregation" do not ensure that Black children learn; such goals do ensure that Black children will be in the minority in every school. These goals do ensure that Black children will continue to be oppressed by the white-controlled racist school system.

Barbara Sizemore said in her testimony before the Mondale Committee that the first *Brown* decision was racist because it implied that segregation does no harm to white children, segregated schools are seen as good schools for whites. She said, "If an institution supports the folk who give the inference of authority to another folk, how can that institution help the so-called inferior folk?"

Black children today are very different from the Black children of 1954. To tell a Black child today that he will profit by sitting next to a white child in a white-controlled school is to lie to him. And he knows it. The only thing that child will gain is more knowledge of white racism. This is a learning experience for him but it does not help him learn how to read and write.

In light of this, and in light of the student's "rights" which have been shown to exist only in theory, three points can be made about busing children for "racial balance":

First, it appears that busing insures that Black children will always be in the minority, thus providing an ideal climate for racist practices to continue.

Second, the terms "busing," "desegregation," and "racial balance" are used by the power elite in this country to keep poor whites and poor Blacks from joining together to demand a decent life and the right to survive. If the people who are paid to educate children don't do it, what better way to divert attention from their failures than by stirring up the folks, calling poor whites "racists" and forcing both white and Black to go to a school in which no one will ever learn anyway?

Third, "racial balance" is used to curtail the authority of Black teachers and administrators. In Dayton, the community word is that, in balancing the staff of the schools to a 70-30 ratio, the good Black teachers went to the white schools and the incompetent white teachers came to the Black schools.

Because of these effects of "desegregation," it is a denial of a Black student's right to an education to move him to a white school. We are putting the burden on children, both Black and white, to eradicate the mental illness of 300 years in American society. This "racial balance" is easy for the power elite to support because it puts the burden on the children, not on their own racist shoulders where it belongs. True integration, as Sizemore says, would bring about an open society in which segregated housing, economic racism on all levels, and unequal educational and medical services would be eliminated.

I believe in freedom of choice for Black people. If Black parents wish to send their children to white schools, the law should facilitate that wish. If, however, Black parents, having developed a sense of nationalism and racial pride, decide that Black-controlled schools would better educate their children, the law should protect that decision.

As I see it, when we talk about busing we are talking about institutionalized racism. And I believe that urban schools are merely an extension of the slave system. In many respects Black people are still enslaved. In many respects, *poor* people are enslaved. In many respects all oppressed people are enslaved.

Do you think it's possible for Blacks and oppressed white people to join together in a common struggle?

There has to be some kind of cooperation and understanding between poor white and poor Black students. I think that if there is racial violence in this country, initially it would not be between middle-class Black and middle-class white people; it would be between poor white people and poor Black people, and they are both oppressed in many of the same ways.

I have been through an experience where I had to rescue some Black children from a white Appalachian school. One strategy would be to be angry with poor white folks for the rest of my life, but another strategy would be to understand that *they* are oppressed in many of the same ways Black people are oppressed. In many ways they are victims of the news media and victims of the powerful and the rich. I am not saying that poor white people and poor Black people have to love each other, but I am saying they have to get together on things that they agree on to prevent potential genocide of both. I think that that can be done, not by what some expert says, but by giving them power and giving them some money and letting them make their own decision about how they can relate together and how they can live together.

I agree with Lerone Bennett, however, when he talks about the fact that you have to be strong before you go into any coalition. Black folks have been ripped off time and time again in coalition situations. The emphasis has to be on Black folks getting together with Black folks first and poor whites getting themselves together too. The immediate strategy with white folks has to be one of peaceful coexistence.

I think the same thing's happening within the public schools that happened during slavery. For example, during slavery Black people were told that we were dumb, that we were dirty, that we were silly, that we were thieves. That gave us a negative feeling of self. How does the institution called school work? The institution calls students socially disadvantaged, culturally deprived—now don't think that those terms don't have ramifications in terms of how teachers deal with those students, how administrators administrate for those students, how other institutions that are serving those students *view* those students. The institution also stereotypes to cover up its failure, to cover up its inability to produce. Earl Kelly said it very clearly—adults always blame powerless children for their inadequacies. Institutions always find a scapegoat for the fact that they can't produce, or that they are deliberately not producing.

It sounds like there's no way out.

That's what the oppressor wants us to believe. In this country today, Black men who want to be men have few alternatives. We can go to Algiers, we can end up in jail, we can end up destroyed psychologically or physically if we stand up for our rights. In my own case, the Stivers High School incident documented by Dr. Ruth W. Burgin in the book, *An Experiment in Community School Control: An Evaluation of the Dayton Experience,* speaks of a form of genocide, a form that seeks to eliminate Black men from positions of power or potential power. As a result of incidents of this kind, young Black and other oppressed people are forced into despair. Many feel, "Why learn and why study when in a few years I'm going to be destroyed anyway?"

There is a growing concern among Black educators and community leaders that, since there is no more cotton to pick and there are no more ditches to dig, Blacks as a people are no longer necessary to this country, especially in view of the population control themes being developed. Some believe that the billions of dollars being pumped into programs like the Title I Elementary and Secondary Education Act to provide funds for assistance to so-called educationally disadvantaged children are merely being used to prove the racist theory of genetic inferiority of Black children, as espoused by men like Jensen. The argument runs something like this: "You see, we have given billions and look, those children still cannot learn."

How does this oppression actually work itself out in the school?

The school is a certified agent of oppression. There are many similarities between urban schools that I've been associated with and Attica. At Attica they shot people down physically; in the public schools they shoot children down psychologically. The result is the same, death. In fact, as Dr. Martin Luther King stated, psychological death can be even more painful than physical death. Let me give you an example. This nine-year-old brother was watching the Today show. He was Black. A very brilliant Black Ph.D. was on the show. The young brother didn't understand what the Ph.D. was talking about. But he was impressed by his sharp clothes and the fact that he was on television. He ran to school. He was late because he had been watching the Today show. He asked his teacher, "How much money do it cost to be a doctor, so I can be on television and be like that man I saw on television, and be sharp, and be talking like he was talking?" His teacher told him, "Sit down—sit down because you don't have enough money to be thinking about school and you can't read anyway." He was nine years old. He didn't come to school the next day. He started stealing little petty stuff, hub caps, routine stuff. Then he started getting into more serious trouble. Then he started becoming aggressive in social situations. He eventually got into serious trouble—and he is, in fact, doing time now for a very serious crime.

You can multiply that example in one form or another for every child who gets trapped in the general course, or gets pushed out of a college preparatory course, or learns how to sit in class and be a good "boy" or good "girl" and graduates, but can't read. Or gets pushed out of school.

What are the consequences of being in the general course?

Counselors are among the greatest violators of the equal protection granted to all people under the United States Constitution. They can deprive children of this protection with one statement: "You are not smart enough to take the college preparatory course."

When a counselor makes this statement, he often deprives the student of a good job, good housing, good medical treatment, and a happy and healthy life. If the student doesn't drop out, he winds up in another dead end—the general course.

You take a student in an academic course and ask him what he wants to be. He'll say: a doctor, a lawyer, a chemist. You ask a student in the business course what he wants to be and he'll tell you an office manager, a banker, a real estate man, a salesman. Ask a student attending one of the few good vocational schools what he wants to be and he will say a draftsman or machinist.

You ask a student in the general course what he wants to be and he'll say, "I dunno." I look at the classified want ads in the Dayton papers every day and I see ads for all kinds of jobs. But I don't see any ads for "General Jobs."

The general course is a combined concentration camp, babysitting service, and mental graveyard. It is excellent preparation for the future junkies of America, the future jobless of America.

The general course, like the poor conditions of performance and services and supplies and material resources in Black and other oppressed communities, exists not by chance, but by design. I think that those of us who are in constant contact with the people who are suffering in this country must repeat and repeat and repeat the essence of that suffering—institutionalized racism.

I have personal experience with how teachers try to program Black children into failure. The one lesson that I learned well in junior high school only took about two minutes to teach and I have never forgotten it. A math teacher told me that I would never be any good, that I was dumb, and that I would never finish school. I believe today that I made up my mind right then and there to make a damn liar out of him.

Now he told my best friend the same thing, and that friend didn't see that it was the system that was no good—he believed it was him. For shortly after that teacher hit my friend with the same cruel, harsh, and criminal words, my friend started staying away from school, getting in trouble and is, in fact, in trouble today, serious trouble. He is in jail. As far as I am concerned—whatever crime my friend is accused of—the teacher who made that statement to him way back in 1950 is equally guilty and should be serving the same time under the same conditions.

Now, I had a sense of what was happening, but it was still very hard for me. Because of some racist IQ test, when I got to high school, my mother had to spend about three weeks convincing white folks that I should take the college preparatory course. When she finally fought hard enough for me to get into the college preparatory course, they had already psychologically destroyed my will to take algebra and geometry

In questions of student violations of school rules, the student, like any citizen, should be regarded as innocent until proven guilty. The burden of proof should rest with the school. The student has a right to full due process of law.... When discipline is arbitrary, as it is, for the most part, now, it prepares students to live in a society where they will have no control over forces that affect their lives. It encourages an acceptance of impotence, an acceptance of the individual's inability to change a given situation. It is time to give students the constitutional rights they already, in theory, have—including the important right to a fair trial in questions of rule violations.

—Recommendation from the Dayton Student Board of Inquiry into High School Discipline.

and all college subjects. So when I went into those college preparatory courses I went in there with the feeling—"I can't really do this because the teacher said I couldn't do it, and the counselor said I couldn't do it, and the principal said I couldn't do it, and the assistant superintendent of the district said I couldn't do it. I must be stupid."

But my main point is that by making sure that most Black children end up in the general course with no belief that they can do or be anything else, the system is committing psychological genocide and perhaps even getting ready for physical genocide. There's hardly a chance that any of *us* are going to be in positions to control the new technologies—those that may mean the difference between survival and death. You have to think seriously about why our children aren't being trained for the future.

Do you want to start educating children for the future or for dealing, first of all, with their present condition?

One without the other is meaningless. Right now we should be teaching children how to make their own worlds more livable. They should learn about legal redress against slum landlords. They should learn about taxes and how they are levied. They should learn consumer law and credit and how to protect themselves in the marketplace. They should learn about due process so that they can protect themselves and their parents from a society that does not look kindly on them.

Besides this, our children must be schooled in the future. We must have architects who can plan low-cost housing. We must have children who can learn oceanography and assure our people a place in submarine communities. We have seen from experience that the white establishment will leave its decaying cities to Black people while fleeing into the suburbs. They will not automatically, out of brotherhood, indulge in integrated submarine communities. Our children must be taught about space flight—so that they will not be left on a pollution-clogged earth while whites hit the moon and beyond. Black children must learn the new medicine so that their children will not be used as spare parts when some white man needs a heart. Our children must learn genetics so that the race is not bred out of existence when the era of test-tube babies becomes a reality. Our children must learn about psychology and the media so that they will not be manipulated back into slavery.

Instead of the general course, why not substitute a curriculum that produces skilled craftsmen in oceanography, genetic research, atomic fusion, chemistry and biology, medicine, computer science, machine design, the media, urban space planning, agronomy, economic planning, and political science as it applies to design models for the survival and liberation of oppressed peoples?

Black people, in the eyes of many people in this country, are no longer necessary. I'm especially pessimistic after reading Sam Yette's brilliant book, *The Choice*. There he deals with *The Issue of Black Survival in America*, the reality that our people are considered obsolete by racists because there is no more cotton to pick, and there are no more ditches to dig. And I see the school as an agency that initiates and perpetuates genocide.

Concentration camps are public schools. Public schools are prisons. You never really do get out of school—because the oppression that you endure during that school day follows you all through your life. When people start talking about population explosion—when they start talking about the density of population, when they start talking about there not being enough resources to feed people—they're talking about getting rid of somebody. Now that's a reality! The majority group, on the basis of its proven record, damn sure doesn't want to volunteer to be eliminated.

Suppose, for example, some high-level government official would say "The environment is so critical that we have to eliminate 25 million folks immediately in order for all of us to continue to breathe. Now would you suggest that we rip off 25 million white folk over 75, if we have that many? Or would you suggest that we just eliminate 25 million Black folks." What would the answer be?

It's easy for white people to say that's paranoid. Many Germans probably said the same thing in Germany just before many Jewish people were destroyed. Black psychiatrists Grier and Cobb point out in *Black Rage* that if a man is Black in America and is not paranoid, he is not normal. It's as normal for a Black man to be paranoid in America as it is for a banker to be prudent or a hunter to be cunning.

Given the fact that the "sane" Black person must acknowledge the psychological genocide that exists and the physical genocide that is possible, what has to happen now, as you see it?

I have to deal with that question on several different levels. One initial step might be to deal directly with the oppressive school-connected agents of genocide. A group of Black educators suggested just recently that we provide school people with two alternatives: either say (1) our children are genetically inferior, or (2) you do not have the ability to educate them.

Most oppressive educators have trouble dealing with those alternatives because even though they *believe* in the genetic inferiority of Black children, they would be reluctant to admit to others that they do not have the capacity to educate our children because that would mean they would no longer be necessary in our schools or in our communities. They would no longer be able to use our children for the purpose of making a living.

If oppressive educators admit that they cannot educate our children, that would mean that they should no longer have access to Black children and other poor and oppressed children. If they no longer had access to our children they would not be able to deliberately destroy them psychologically for the purpose of protecting the myth of white superiority and the reality of institutionalized racism.

To prevent psychological genocide of Black, Chicano, Puerto Rican, Indian, poor and oppressed children, we must remove them from the physical and psychological control of the oppressor. We must also teach them to protect and defend themselves while at the same time not copying the cruel and vicious tactics of the oppressor.

On another level, some of the most brilliant people alive are Black people who have become political prisoners because of the events of the 1960's and 1970's. They possess the insight and the love for their fellow man to deal effectively with the issue of "bringing us together." I believe that legislation should be introduced to grant amnesty to all those who are currently incarcerated because they have fought for the human and constitutional rights of their fellow man. I suggest that they be employed to work toward making this a truly open, democratic society.

Everett Reimer in *School Is Dead* says that, despite the record, the possibility for democratic institutions remains —men, however, must make up their minds to use institutions for democratic purposes. In order to avoid genocide for some and in order to make democracy a reality for all, we must start practicing what we preach from the womb to the tomb, from the pre-schooler to the Supreme Court justice, to the Congressman.

Everett Reimer contends, of course, that school is dead. He may be right. While it is being buried, however, children are still being destroyed.

We must protect our children by any and all means necessary. For example, the local, state, and federal governments of this country have the responsibility of stopping the psychological and physical genocide that is occurring through the schools, the media, health care, drugs, housing, and law enforcement. We must hold individuals who are responsible for racism within the educational system accountable for their actions by initiating criminal court actions or through para-legal avenues of arbitration. We must institute specific programs to develop positive self-image. The Black, poor, and oppressed must be told repeatedly that they are good, they are beautiful, they can do anything they make up their minds to do. Like Huey P. Newton says, "The will of the People is greater than the Man's technology." We must redistribute money, knowledge, and power, and provide alternatives through community-controlled schools, free schools, welfare rights schools, university-run schools, student-run schools, computer-centered schools, schools without walls, home-based schools, etc. We must reform the decision-making bodies of public education to include students between the ages of seven and seventeen with full rights and responsibilities. We must institute student fact-finding commissions—like the Center's recent models, the Student Boards of Inquiry into discipline and into curriculum—to deal with racial issues, discipline, curriculum, guidance, and all other areas of public education. We must federally fund student groups to initiate their own programs relative to rights and responsibilities and education in general—programs, for example, where students help the blind, the poor, the aged. We must federally fund programs for "Black militants," conservative white, Chicano, Puerto Rican, Indian, poor, and oppressed students, so that they can develop their own strategies for peaceful co-existence and survival.

We must strive to make Oscar Handlin's definition of integration a reality. That definition, as interpreted by Barbara Sizemore, is that condition of society in which any individual has the opportunity to make a multitude of voluntary or involuntary contacts with any other human being based on his own preference, taste, or ability. This definition, rather than racial balance, must be our goal. We must federally

School security guards should definitely have more requirements than simply "a clean record" to be placed in a school situation. There should be some history of work with young people, and some intensive training on how to relate to young people under potentially dangerous or explosive conditions. Security guard power in a school should be specifically outlined in writing. Guards should be held personally and professionally accountable for any violations of their written powers.

—Recommendation from the Dayton Student Board of Inquiry into High School Discipline.

fund TV, cable TV, and radio networks throughout this country that can broadcast information to the masses of oppressed people about student rights, welfare rights, and the right to believe in oneself and to love, trust, and respect oneself and others; we must also broadcast the information necessary to eliminate racism, poverty and oppression, and genocide. Although federal grants for compensatory education have failed in the past because money was given to the same racist administrators to help Black children whom they had failed to educate in regular programs, massive expenditures of money could aid Black education—if it were distributed properly, and controlled by the local community, not by the state or the school system.

We must also abolish corporal punishment.

How is it possible to finance these programs?

How is it possible to finance wars? How is it possible to subsidize large corporations? How was it possible to rebuild Germany and Japan?

A number of ideas on how to use such grants have been expressed in Dayton a number of times by myself and others. The ideas were recently re-stated one more time, by the Dayton superintendent who fired me three years ago for developing these same programs.

These ideas include: federal grants used for rent or loan supplements for all poor people—once housing is available to all in all parts of the cities, true integration may be possible. Federal grants for clothing allowances for poor children—the type of clothes a student wears significantly affect teacher attitudes toward the student, and therefore that student's performance. Federal grants for medical and dental service for every poor child—this money could erase some of the outside factors that hinder a poor child's learning. Federal grants to provide part-time jobs for all poor children 12 years and over—if a child can earn his own spending money, he will be less apt to drop out of school. Federal grants for paid transportation either to a special course or a job opportunity for all these children. Federal grants for green space and good playground equipment for all inner-city schools—to alleviate at least the appearance of inner-city schools as prisons. Federal grants for educational travel, camping, and environmental exploration by inner-city pupils.

Then do you feel that such programs could profoundly alter the fate of Black and other oppressed people in this country? Is this the kind of revolution you hope for?

No program for change and liberation can be successful, truly successful, in making equality and democracy a reality unless the people are involved from the beginning. I believe that the only real revolution that can take place in this country, and indeed in this world, is a revolution of peace—love, trust, and respect for each other. There is nothing revolutionary about Black folks and young folks dying in this country. Life is a very precious and dear thing. We have, in this country, made dying as routine as going to the bathroom, and that is a shame. We must somehow emphasize the importance of living and developing strategies to see to it that our young are able to develop to the fullest of their potential. To strive for anything less is to say that all of the Black people who have bled and suffered and died, and all the young people who have bled and suffered and died, have done so for nothing.

I hope Reich is correct in terms of the *Greening of America,* but I believe Sam Yette is correct in terms of *The Choice: The Issue of Black Survival in America.*

In her book, *If They Come in the Morning,* our beautiful, brilliant, and courageous sister Angela Davis states that her life is at stake and that it is not just an individual life but a life that has been given to her people in the struggle against poverty and racism.

James Baldwin, in his letter to Angela Davis, says, "We must fight for your life as though it were our own because if they take you in the morning they will be coming for us that night."

Angela Davis is on trial, Black people are on trial, oppressed people are on trial, and the potential for democracy is on trial. For the sake of our children and for the sake of us all, I hope Angela wins, I hope Black people win, I hope the oppressed win, I hope democracy wins.

We must trust each other. In the end, the oppressed will save themselves and their oppressors. The children, if we allow them to be human, will lead the way.

Footnotes

[1] Tinker v. Des Moines Independent School District, 393 U.S. 503, 89 S. Ct. 733 (1969). This decision is discussed in Richard L. Berkman, "Students in Court: Free Speech and the Functions of Schooling in America," *Harvard Educational Review,* 40 (November, 1970), pp. 567-595.

[2] Serrano v. Priest, 5 Cal. 3rd 584 (1971). The text of this decision is published with commentary by William N. Greenbaum, *Harvard Educational Review,* 41 (November, 1971), pp. 501-534.

[3] The interview took place in Cambridge, Massachusetts in February, 1972. Interviewers were John Butler, Margaret Marshall, Tom Marx, and Ellen Solomon of *HER*. New developments of the Center are discussed in the Editor's Note on p. 163.

[4] While the Center has received grants from the Office of Economic Opportunity, Washington, D.C., 20506, the opinions expressed here are those of Arthur E. Thomas and should not be construed as representing the opinions or policy of any agency of the United States Government.

Sources

My mother—who taught me at an early age to always remember that whenever I saw someone who was suffering or oppressed, "there but for the grace of God, go you." She told me that I should always try to help them, because, were it not for oppression, they would be able to help themselves.

My wife—who is brilliant, Black, and beautiful and best described by Isaac Hayes on the record *Black Moses* in the song "Brand New Me."

Ms. Wilhelmina Robinson, Dr. Ames Chapman, Mr. Isaac Sappe Lane, professors Central State University, Wilberforce, Ohio—they taught me and many others that we were not dumb and that we could learn.

Mrs. Margaret Irby, teacher, Dayton Public Schools; my students; the Black community of Dayton—who taught me and many others to always strive to love, trust, respect, and protect our children and our people.

Ms. Jean Camper Cahn and Dr. Edgar S. Cahn—who helped us fight the racist, oppressive school administration of Dayton at the risk of their lives—and who were instrumental in the development of the Student Rights Center.

Dr. Ruth W. Burgin—who helped us fight the racist, oppressive, school administration of Dayton with the courage of Harriet Tubman and the brilliance of Angela Davis.

Black scholar-educator-activists—who have assisted us with ideas, inspiration, cooperation, assistance, protection, and support: Brother Kenneth Haskins, Brother Preston Wilcox, Dr. Donald H. Smith, Dr. Ermon O. Hogan, Dr. Charles H. Smith, Dr. Bernard C. Watson, Sister Barbara Sizemore, Dr. Rhody McCoy, Dr. Oscar Mims, Brother Julius Hobson, Dr. Gloria Joseph, and many, many others.

Organizations and individuals who have played a major role in the development of the Center: the Model Cities Planning Council of Dayton, the Dayton Community School Councils, Dr. Michael Kantor, Mr. Terry Lenzner, Ms. Patricia Clarkson, Mr. Stephen Huber, Mr. Bruce Kirschenbaum, Mr. Elliott Stanley, Ms. Nancy Stanley, Mr. Donnie Moore, Ms. Marcia Brockenborough, Mr. Troy Overby.

The Student Rights Center Staff: Mr. Peter M. Rebold, Ms. Ruthetta Bankston, Ms. Carol Towarnicky, Ms. Maddi Breslin, Ms. Lillian Meeks, Ms. Lori Tannenbaum.

Ombudsmen—Mr. Edward Campbell, Rev. David Gilbert, Ms. Elizabeth Robinson, Ms. Betty Moore, Ms. Corine Tucker, Ms. Mable Wiley, Ms. Judy Mathis, Mr. Robert Turner, Mr. James Phillips, Mr. Ellis Jacobs, Ms. Gail Stewart, Carroll Boswell.

Some of our best friends are white: the late Charles Bridge—our lawyer, who labored unselfishly against racism, oppression, and injustice; Dr. Larry Hillman, Dr. Arthur Eve, Dr. James H. Pelley, Mr. Albert Rosenberg, Mr. Ray Hruschka, Dr. Neal Shedd, Mr. Gregory Favre.

Records—"Save the Children" as performed by Marvin Gaye, *What's Going On;* "Reach Out and Touch (Somebody's Hand)" as performed by Aretha Franklin, *Live at Fillmore West;* "The Impossible Dream," as performed by Roberta Flack, *Chapter Two,* "Martin Luther King at Zion Hill," "Malcolm X Talks to the Grassroots," "Malcolm X: Ballots or Bullets," "I am Somebody," Rev. Jesse Jackson, *The Country Preacher;* "To Be Young, Gifted, and Black," as sung by Nina Simone, *Black Gold.*

Periodicals—*Ebony* Magazine, *Jet* Magazine, *The Black Scholar, Mohammad Speaks.*

Cahn, Edgar S. and Jean Camper, "The Sovereign Immunity," *Harvard Law Review,* 81 (March, 1968).

Cahn, Edgar S. and Jean Camper, "Power to the People or the Profession?—the Public Interest in Public Interest Law," *The Yale Law Journal,* Vol. 79 (May, 1970).

Cahn, Edgar S. and Jean Camper, "The War on Poverty: A Civilian Perspective," *The Yale Law Journal,* 73 (July 1964).

"Mondale Commission Report": *Equal Educational Opportunity Hearings Before the Select Committee on Equal Educational Opportunity of the United States Senate, Ninety-Second Congress:* First Session, Part 13. Washington, D.C.: Government Printing Office, 1971.

Poussaint, Alvin, "A Psychiatrist Looks at Black Power," *Ebony* (March, 1969).

Thomas, Arthur E., and Ruth W. Burgin. *Community School Council, Philosophy and Framework for Urban Educational Change.* Wilberforce, Ohio: Institute for Research and Development in Urban Areas, Central State University, May, 1971.

Thomas, Arthur E. *Delinquency: An Assessment of the Juvenile Delinquency Prevention and Control Act of 1968,* ed. Larry L. Dye, "Love, Trust, and Respect for Each Other, Preconditions of Justice as the Basis for Law and Order." Amherst, Mass.: University of Massachusetts Conference, 1970.

Thomas, Arthur E. and Ruth W. Burgin. *An Experiment in Community School Control: An Evaluation of the Dayton Experience.* Wilberforce, Ohio: Institute for Research and Development in Urban Areas. Central State University, May 1971.

Monographs

Banks, James A. and Grambs, Jean D. ed. *Black Self-Concept.* New York: McGraw-Hill, 1972.

Bennett, Lerone, Jr. *Before the Mayflower.* Baltimore: Penguin, 1966.

The Challenge of Blackness. Chicago: Johnson Publishing, 1972.

Carmichael, Stokeley and Hamilton, Charles V. *Black Power: The Politics of Liberation in America.* New York: Vintage Books, Alfred A. Knopf, 1967.

Davis, Angela Y. *If They Come in the Morning.* New York: Joseph Okpaku Publishing, 1971.

Fader, Daniel. *The Naked Children.* New York: Macmillan, 1971.

Fanon, Frantz. *The Wretched of the Earth.* New York: Grove Press, 1968.

———. *Toward the African Revolution.* New York: Grove Press, 1967.

Freire, Paulo. *The Pedagogy of the Oppressed.* New York: Herder and Herder, 1971.

Friedenberg, Edgar. *Coming of Age in America.* New York: Random House, 1965.

Green, Robert L. *Racial Crisis in American Education.* Chicago: Follett Educational, 1969.

Hogan, Ermon O., "Racism in Education: A Barrier to Quality Education," Chapter 7 in Green, *Racial Crisis in American Education.*

Illich, Ivan. *Deschooling Society.* New York: Harper and Row, 1971.

Kelley, Earl C. *In Defense of Youth.* Englewood Cliffs, N.J.: Prentice-Hall, 1962.

Lurie, Ellen. *How to Change the Schools.* New York: Random House, 1971.

Malcolm X. "To Mississippi Youth." *Malcolm X Speaks.* Edited by George Breitman. New York: Grove Press, 1965.

McKissick, Floyd. *Three-fifths of a Man.* New York: Macmillan, 1969.

Reich, Charles A. *The Greening of America.* New York: Random House, 1971.

Reimer, Everett. *School is Dead.* Garden City, N.Y: Doubleday and Co., 1970, 1971.

Ryan, William B. *Blaming the Victim.* New York: Pantheon Books, Random House, 1971.

Toffler, Alvin. *Future Shock.* New York: Random House, 1970.

Wright, Nathan, Jr., ed. *What Black Educators Are Saying.* New York: Hawthorne Books, 1970.

Yette, Samuel F. *The Choice: The Issue of Black Survival in America.* New York: G. P. Putnam's Sons, 1971.

Center Publications

Faust, Ralph and Thomas, Arthur E., *Student Rights Handbook for Dayton, Ohio,* prepared by the Center for the Study of Student Citizenship, Rights, and Responsibilities. Dayton, Ohio and the National Juvenile Law Center, St. Louis, Missouri, September, 1971.

Geringer, Dan, "The Devil Made Me Suspend That Boy," *Rap Magazine,* June, 1971.

Geringer, Dan, ed. "Three Nights in Dayton," a special section of *Rap Magazine,* October, 1971.

Thomas, Arthur E., "Can They Do These Things to Us?," *Rap Magazine,* November, 1971.

Thomas, Arthur E. and Towarnicky, Carol, "Of Scapegoats and Other Healthy Animals," *Rap Magazine,* December, 1971.

Towarnicky, Carol, ed., "Juvenile Rights in Ohio," a special section of *Rap Magazine,* March, 1971.

Towarnicky, Carol, "Respect Each Other, Be Real Nice," *Rap Magazine,* January, 1971.

Towarnicky, Carol, ed., "What We Study and Why," a special section of *Rap Magazine,* April 1972.

Copies may be ordered directly from Arthur E. Thomas, the Bolinga Black Cultural Resources Center, Wright State University, Dayton, Ohio 45431.

Appendix

The following are sections of the Ohio Revised Code. Most states have similar laws which have never been applied to educators and the education system. Because of the novelty of the proposed use for these laws, it might be difficult for citizens to swear out warrants against educators, and for prosecutors to prosecute violations of these laws. Such use of these laws may be a few years away, but citizens may have to resort to the criminal law, and use it in the way proposed here, to force constructive change in the education of our children—A.E.T.

ORC 2919.05—Embezzlement by Municipal and School Officers

"No member of the council of a municipal corporation, or an officer, agent, or employee of a municipal corporation, or board of education, shall knowingly divert, appropriate, or apply funds raised by taxation or otherwise, to any use or purpose other than that for which said funds were raised or appropriated, or knowingly divert, appropriate, or apply money borrowed, or a bond of the municipal corporation or part of the proceeds of such bond, to any use or purpose other than that for which such loan was made, or bond issued. Whoever violates this section shall be . . . imprisoned not less than one nor more than twenty-one years."

ORC 2919.05—Usurpation of Office

"No person in an office or place of authority without being lawfully authorized to do so, or by color of his office shall willfully oppress another under pretense of acting in his official capacity.

"Whoever violates this section shall be fined not more than two hundred dollars."

Boards of education and educators willfully defraud parents when they say they are educating their children. Children are willfully oppressed by the educational system.

ORC 2911.41—Fraudulent Advertising

"No person shall directly or indirectly make, publish, disseminate, circulate, or place before the public, in this state, in a newspaper, magazine, or other publication, or in the form of a book, notice, handbill, poster-circular, pamphlet, letter, sign, placard, card, label, or over any radio station, or in any other way, an advertisement or announcement of any sort regarding merchandise, securities, service, employment, real estate, or anything of value offered by him for use, purchase, or sale and which advertisement or announcement, contains any assertion, representation, or statement which is untrue, or fraudulent.

Whoever violates this section shall be fined not more than two hundred dollars or imprisoned not more than twenty days or both."

Are not boards of education and educators guilty of violations of this law? Is not every school tax levy campaign a violation? School people advertise education. Children and parents are consumers of education induced by false advertising.

ORC 2907.21—Larceny by Trick

"No person shall obtain possession of, or title to, anything of value without the consent of the person from whom he obtained it, provided he did not induce such consent by false or fraudulent representation, pretense, token, or writing.

"Whoever violates this section is guilty of larceny by trick, and, if the value of the thing so obtained is sixty dollars or more, shall be imprisoned not less than one nor more than seven years.

School boards and administrators have been taking public money for years with public consent. Indeed, they ask for more and more money. The public consent is induced by representations made by administrators that children's education will improve, and the pretense that children learn in proportion to the dollars spent. These representations are false. The proof of their falsity is that high school diplomas are awarded to people who read and write at an eighth grade level.

ORC 2903.08—Torturing or Neglecting Children

"No person having the control of . . . a child under the age of sixteen years shall willfully . . . torture, torment, or cruelly or unlawfully punish him . . .

Whoever violates this section shall be fined no less than ten nor more than two hundred dollars or imprisoned not more than six months, or both."

School systems claim to have control of children during school hours. Willful torture and torment occurs when children are harassed and molded to conform to the system's model of the perfect student. To keep a child in school eight hours a day, listening to a teacher who says nothing relevant, is cruel punishment.

ORC Section 2901.12—Robbery

"No person by force or violence, or by putting in fear, shall steal from the person of another anything of value.

"Whoever violates this section is guilty of robbery, and shall be imprisoned not less than one nor more than twenty-five years."

Our system of education puts children in fear, and steals from them their desire to learn, their inquiring minds, and their individuality.

ORC 2921.14—Conspiracy to Defraud the State

"If two or more persons conspire to defraud this state, or any political subdivision thereof, in any manner, or for any purpose, and one or more of such parties do any act to effect the object of the conspiracy, each of the parties to such conspiracy shall be fined not more than five thousand dollars or imprisoned not more than two years, or both."

Photographs on page 195 were taken by Al Wilson of the *Journal Herald,* Dayton, Ohio, and are used here by permission. All other photographs were taken by Lori Tanenbaum, staff member of the Students Rights Center. *HER* is grateful to Ms. Tanenbaum for her extensive help and advice. We also wish to thank Ms. Cynthia Brady for her sustaining work in lay-out and design.

Editor's Note: The Center for the Study of Student Citizenship, Rights, and Responsibilities has enlarged to become the West Dayton Youth Services Bureau, a division of the United Fund. Directed by one of Thomas's former students, it is now open on a 24-hour basis and is replicated in other cities throughout the United States in a network of youth service bureaus. Some of the original parent ombudsmen now operate a student advocacy center at the University of Dayton on a volunteer basis.

Notes on Contributors

FRANK ADAMS, a member of the Board of Directors of the Highlander Research and Education Center, New Market, Tennessee, is author of *Unearthing Seeds of Fire: The Idea of Highlander* (1975). His research interests include anarchist educational history and theory, and he is presently at work on *The Broken Paddle: Limits of Authority in Anarchist Education*. He is also a farmer, truck driver, newsman, cobbler, weaver, and woodcarver.

CENTER FOR NEW SCHOOLS (CNS) is a non-profit organization working to improve the quality of urban public education and to make public schools more responsive to the communities they serve. CNS assists parents, students, teachers, administrators, and other community members who wish to create fundamental changes in existing schools or to set up new schools within public school systems. CNS staff members have been key planners and consultants in the development of Metro High School, an alternative "high school without walls" operating within the Chicago public school system. CNS publications, documenting their research and other projects, can be obtained from the Center for New Schools, Suite 1800, 59 East Van Buren, Chicago, Illinois 60695.

HERBERT GINTIS is Associate Professor of Economics at the University of Massachusetts, Amherst. Formerly Assistant Professor of Economics at Harvard University and Lecturer at the Harvard Graduate School of Education, his research interests include Marxism and the political economy of education. He is co-author with Samuel Bowles of *Schooling in Capitalist America: Educational Reform and the Contradictions of Economic Life* (1975).

DENIS GOULET, author of numerous articles and books, has most recently written *A New Moral Order: Development Ethics and Liberation Theology* (1974) and is presently writing a book on value conflicts in international technology transfers. Dr. Goulet has been a Visiting Fellow at the Center for the Study of Democratic Institutions, Santa Barbara, California and at the Center for the Study of Development and Social Change, Cambridge, Massachusetts. He has served as a development planning advisor in Lebanon and Brazil and currently is a Visiting Fellow at the Overseas Development Council, Washington, D.C.

ROBERT C. RIORDAN has worked for five years as a teacher/advisor, administrator, and consultant at the Cambridge Pilot School, an urban, alternative public school-within-a-school.

He is a doctoral candidate in Learning Environments at the Harvard Graduate School of Education and is author of *Alternative Schools in Action* (1972).

ARTHUR E. THOMAS is at Wright State University as Director of the Bolinga Black Cultural Resources Center and Assistant Professor of Post Graduate and Continuing Education, the School of Medicine. Author of numerous articles and essays, he has been a consultant to the U.S. Department of Health, Education and Welfare, the Office of Education, and the National Institute for Education.